# MUSIC THEORY
## FOR
# BEGINNERS

Emma Danes
Designed by Rebecca Halverson
Illustrated by Gerald Wood

Consultant: Katie Elliott
Edited by Jane Chisholm
With thanks to Eileen O'Brien

# CONTENTS

# INTRODUCTION

Theory is all about how music works and is put together, and how it is written down so that people can understand it. Learning theory is very important for anyone who sings or plays an instrument. It enables you to read music, and to pass on your own musical ideas to other people. Although theory can seem difficult at first, this book explains common signs, symbols and technical words clearly and simply, and will help you to understand and enjoy all kinds of music.

## How to use this book

As you read this book, it will help if you play the examples on a melody instrument or keyboard, so you can hear how they sound. The extracts from pieces by famous composers show you how the things you are learning about are put into practice. Labels also explain extra symbols, or tell you where in the book you can find out about them.

## Test yourself

Try writing down the signs you learn on manuscript paper, and test yourself with the questions you will find down the sides of some of the pages. All the answers are on page 47.

## Looking things up

To find out where a topic is covered, look at the contents list on page 2, or the index on page 48. On each page, words which are defined, and other important words, are in **bold** type, so you can see them at a glance.

There is a list of common symbols on page 46. These have page numbers next to them which tell you where in the book you can find out what they mean.

To look up scales or key signatures, turn to pages 42-43. Musical terms in foreign languages are explained on pages 44-45.

You can find the dates of all the composers whose music appears in this book on page 23.

# THE STAFF AND THE TREBLE CLEF

The exact highness or lowness of a note is called its **pitch**. Tunes are made up of notes of different pitches. You can tell the pitch of a note by the way it is written.

Corelli was the first famous composer who only wrote music for instruments. He was also an important violin teacher.

## The staff

Today music is usually written on a set of five horizontal lines called a **staff**. The notes fit on the lines and in the spaces between them. You read the notes from left to right. As the notes go up toward the top of the staff their pitch gets higher. You can see this on the staff below.

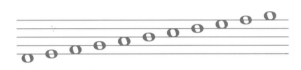

Lower notes                              Higher notes

## Ledger lines

To show notes which are higher or lower than the ones which fit on the staff lines, you add extra short lines, called **ledger lines**, above or below the staff.

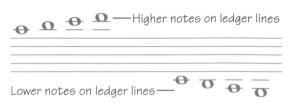

Higher notes on ledger lines

Lower notes on ledger lines

## The treble clef

The pitch of the notes on a staff depends on a sign called a **clef**. One type of clef, the **treble clef**, curls around the second staff line up. A note on this line is G. As the notes move up the staff, their names go alphabetically from A to G. After G, the next note up is A again. The distance from a note to the next note up or down with the same name is called an **octave**.

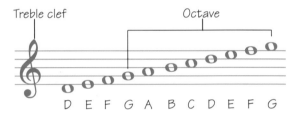

Treble clef                 Octave

D   E   F   G   A   B   C   D   E   F   G

---

## Corelli: *Adagio* (for recorder)

**Staff.** Five horizontal lines on which music is written.

**Treble clef.** A sign which tells you that a note on the second line up is G.

**Note.** The position of a note on the staff, together with the clef, tells you exactly how high or low it sounds.

**Stem.** One of the parts of the note which tells you how long it lasts for (see page 8).

**Notehead.** Can be solid or open. One of the parts of the note which tells you how long it lasts for (see page 8).

The note B.

**Time signature.** Tells you how to count. Find out more on page 10.

**Rest.** Tells you to leave a silence in the music (see page 9).

**Treble clef.** The clef is written on each staff of a piece.

The note F.

**Breath mark.** Tells someone playing a wind instrument, such as a flute or recorder, when to breathe.

The note E.

**Dotted note.** A dot after a note makes it longer (see page 9).

The note C.

**Bar line.** Divides music into small sections called measures. Find out more on page 10.

**Double bar line.** Tells you the music is finished. Find out more on page 10.

4

## Middle C

**Middle C** is the name for the note C which is written on a ledger line just below the staff in the treble clef. On a piano, Middle C is the C nearest to the middle of the keyboard.

Middle C written in the treble clef

## Uses for the treble clef

The treble clef is used for instruments which play lots of notes higher than Middle C, and for high voices, such as treble, soprano and alto. Instruments which use the treble clef include the recorder, flute, clarinet, violin and guitar. Music for the right hand to play on the piano is usually written in the treble clef too. The treble clef is also used for some instruments, such as the viola or cello, when they have very high notes to play.

You can find out about other clefs, and when they are used, on page 6.

## Octave signs

Notes with lots of ledger lines can be difficult to read. Because of this, if there are some very high notes in a piece, an **octave sign** is often used. This tells you that all the notes under the sign *8va* and the horizontal line should be played an octave higher than they are written.

Octave sign and line showing which notes sound an octave higher

Music for the tenor voice is written in the treble clef, but a small eight below the treble clef tells you to sing all the notes an octave lower than written.

The opening of the Mozart song at the bottom of the page, written without the octave sign

This manuscript is in Mozart's handwriting. Mozart worked out musical ideas in detail in his head before he wrote anything down.

> Can you figure out the name of each note in the music by Corelli on page 4?

## Mozart: *Abendempfindung* (for tenor voice)

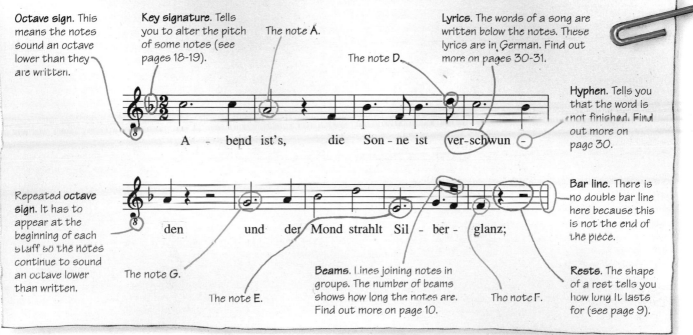

**Octave sign.** This means the notes sound an octave lower than they are written.

**Key signature.** Tells you to alter the pitch of some notes (see pages 18-19).

The note A.

The note D.

**Lyrics.** The words of a song are written below the notes. These lyrics are in German. Find out more on pages 30-31.

**Hyphen.** Tells you that the word is not finished. Find out more on page 30.

A – bend ist's, die Son – ne ist ver-schwun –

**Repeated octave sign.** It has to appear at the beginning of each staff so the notes continue to sound an octave lower than written.

den und der Mond strahlt Sil – ber – glanz;

**Bar line.** There is no double bar line here because this is not the end of the piece.

The note G.

The note E.

**Beams.** Lines joining notes in groups. The number of beams shows how long the notes are. Find out more on page 10.

The note F.

**Rests.** The shape of a rest tells you how long it lasts for (see page 9).

# OTHER CLEFS

Any note can be written in the treble clef if you use enough ledger lines. But to make notes easier to read, other clefs are used by instruments which play lots of notes below Middle C.

## The bass clef

The **bass clef** has a dot on either side of the second staff line down. A note on this line is F. You can see the names of the notes written in the bass clef on the staff below.

Bass clef

F G A B C D E F G A B

## The alto clef

The **alto clef** is centered on the middle line of the staff. A note on this line is Middle C. The staff below shows the names of the notes on all the lines and spaces of the staff.

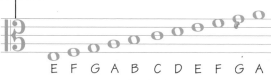

Alto clef

E F G A B C D E F G A

The tuba, bassoon and double bass use the bass clef.

## The tenor clef

The **tenor clef** is centered on the second staff line down. A note on this line is Middle C.

Tenor clef

C D E F G A B C D E F

## Uses for different clefs

The bass clef is used by instruments including the cello, double bass, bassoon and tuba, and by bass singers. Usually it is also used for music to be played with the left hand on the piano.

The alto clef is used by the viola, which plays lower notes than the violin but higher notes than the cello.

The tenor clef is sometimes used by the cello and bassoon, for notes which would need a lot of ledger lines to write out in the bass clef. This means the clef may change during a piece.

---

## J.S. Bach: *Bourrée* (for cello)

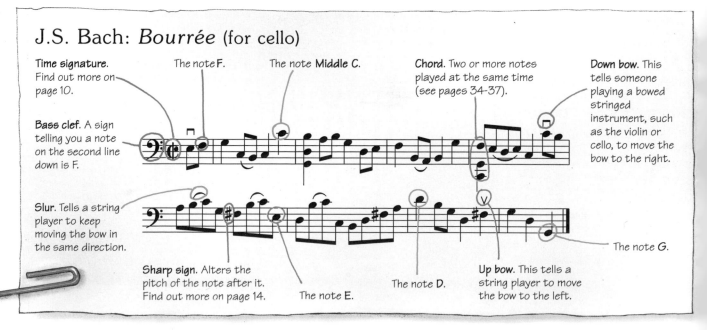

**Time signature.** Find out more on page 10.

The note F.

The note **Middle C**.

**Chord.** Two or more notes played at the same time (see pages 34-37).

**Down bow.** This tells someone playing a bowed stringed instrument, such as the violin or cello, to move the bow to the right.

**Bass clef.** A sign telling you a note on the second line down is F.

**Slur.** Tells a string player to keep moving the bow in the same direction.

**Sharp sign.** Alters the pitch of the note after it. Find out more on page 14.

The note E.

The note D.

**Up bow.** This tells a string player to move the bow to the left.

The note G.

## Fauré: *Berceuse* (for viola)

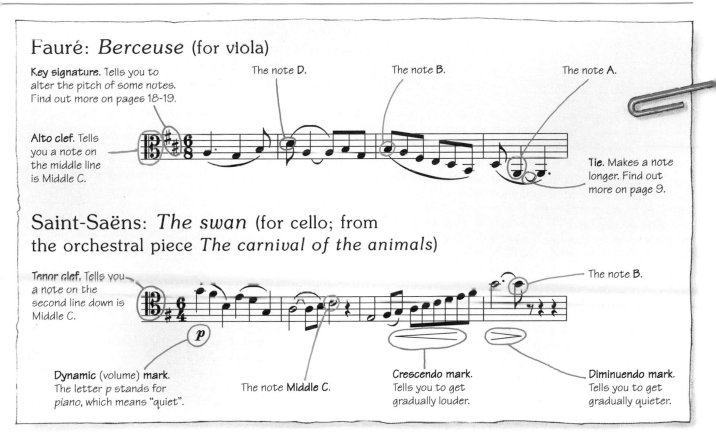

**Key signature.** Tells you to alter the pitch of some notes. Find out more on pages 18-19.

The note D.

The note B.

The note A.

**Alto clef.** Tells you a note on the middle line is Middle C.

**Tie.** Makes a note longer. Find out more on page 9.

## Saint-Saëns: *The swan* (for cello; from the orchestral piece *The carnival of the animals*)

**Tenor clef.** Tells you a note on the second line down is Middle C.

The note B.

*p*

**Dynamic (volume) mark.** The letter *p* stands for *piano*, which means "quiet".

The note **Middle C.**

**Crescendo mark.** Tells you to get gradually louder.

**Diminuendo mark.** Tells you to get gradually quieter.

## More about Middle C

Below you can see four different ways to write Middle C.

These notes all have exactly the same pitch.

## More about octave signs

For very low notes, an **octave sign** is sometimes used, especially in piano music. All the notes above the sign *8va* and the horizontal line sound an octave lower than they are written.

*8va*

Octave sign and line below the staff showing notes sound an octave lower

## Changing a clef

Sometimes it is useful to rewrite music in another clef, perhaps so you can play it on a different instrument. To do this you need to know the names of the notes in each clef, and where Middle C is. Below, you can see the same notes, starting on A below Middle C, written in three clefs.

A  G  B  D  A  A  B  G

A  G  B  D  A  A  B  G

A  G  B  D  A  A  B  G

Can you name each note in the first line of music by J.S. Bach on page 6?

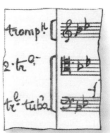

This manuscript by Fauré shows several clefs.

# NOTE LENGTHS

This is a portrait of J.S. Bach. He wrote the piece on this page for his wife, Anna Magdalena.

In most music, each note has to last for a particular length of time. You measure note lengths in steady counts called **beats**. The shape of a note tells you how many beats it lasts for.

## The parts of a note

The oval part of a note which sits on a staff or ledger line is called a **notehead**. Some notes have an upright line joined to the notehead, called a **stem**, and curved lines joining the stem, called **tails**.

An open notehead with no stem or tail is a **whole note**.

A note with a stem and a tail is an **eighth note**.

An open notehead with a stem is a **half note**.

A note with two tails is a **sixteenth note**.

A solid notehead with a stem is a **quarter note**.

A note with three tails is a **thirty-second note**.

## Stem direction

Stems can go up or down. If the notehead is on or above the middle line of the staff, the stem usually goes down. If the notehead is below the middle line, the stem usually goes up.

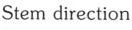

These notes are written correctly.

If the stem goes up you draw it on the right of the notehead. If it goes down you draw it on the left of the notehead. Tails always go to the right.

The *Musette* below would probably have been played on a harpsichord when it was first written.

Notes with tails can be joined together. (Find out more on page 10.) When this happens, make the stems go the way that is right for most of the notes. For two notes, make the stem right for the note farthest from the middle line.

Stems going up      Stems going down

## Note lengths

The chart below shows how different note lengths relate to each other. As you go to the right, each type of note is half as long as the one before.

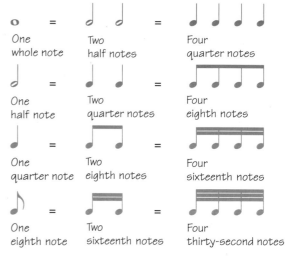

---

# J.S. Bach: *Musette* (for keyboard)

Quarter note.

Stems going down. All these notes are above the middle staff line.

Sixteenth notes.

Slur. Tells you to play smoothly.

Dynamic mark. The letter f stands for *forte*, which means "loud".

Stems going up. These notes are below the middle staff line.

Eighth notes.

Staccato mark. Tells you to make the note short and detached (not joined smoothly to the next note).

## Rests

A silence in music is called a **rest**. You count rests just like notes. For example, a quarter rest is the same length as a quarter note.

▬ Whole rest

▬ Half rest

𝄽 Quarter rest

𝄾 Eighth rest

𝄿 Sixteenth rest

𝅀 Thirty-second rest

## Dotted notes and rests

A **dot** after a note or rest makes it half as long again.

A dotted half note lasts for a half note plus half a half note (a quarter note), or three quarter beats.

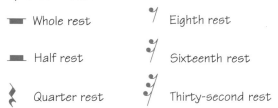

𝅗𝅥. = 𝅗𝅥 + 𝅘𝅥

A dotted quarter rest lasts for a quarter rest plus half a quarter rest (an eighth rest), or three eighth beats.

𝄽. = 𝄽 + 𝄾

## Tied notes

Two or more notes of the same pitch can be joined by a curved line called a **tie**. This makes one note as long as the separate notes added together. The notes do not sound separately.

A quarter note tied to another quarter note lasts for two quarter beats.

A quarter note tied to a half note lasts for three quarter beats.

## Two lines of music on a staff

Some music, for example the piece by Sor at the bottom of this page, has two separate **lines** of music on one staff. The lines are played or sung at the same time. The stems of the top line all go up, and the stems of the bottom line all go down. A note which belongs to both lines of music has two stems, one going up and one going down.

This picture shows the *Soldiers' chorus* scene from a performance of Gounod's *Faust*.

---

## Gounod: *Soldiers' chorus* (from the opera *Faust*)

**Time signature.** Tells you to count in eighth beats. Find out more on page 10.

**Quarter note.**

**Eighth rest.** Lasts for one eighth beat.

**Dotted eighth rest.** Lasts for one and a half eighth beats.

**Tied notes.** Means one note lasts for four eighth beats.

**Dotted half note.** Lasts for six eighth beats.

**Sixteenth note.**

**Dotted quarter note.** Lasts for three eighth beats.

**Eighth note.**

## Sor: *Allegro in C* (for guitar)

Top **line** of music (the tune). All the stems go up.

The two lines of music have different note lengths at the same time.

**Dotted half note.** Lasts for three quarter beats.

**Right-hand fingering.** Tells the player which fingers to play the strings with.

**Left-hand fingering.** Tells the player which fingers to press the strings with.

**Half note.** Lasts for two quarter beats.

**Bottom line** of music (the accompaniment). Stems go down.

# RHYTHMS

A pattern of sounds of particular lengths is called a **rhythm**. In music, rhythms are usually divided into sections called **measures**. This shows which notes are the most important ones, as you will see below, and helps you to count the rhythm.

Debussy often wrote music with very quick, fluid rhythms.

## Measures and bar lines

Music is divided into measures by vertical lines on the staff called **bar lines**. A **double bar line**, with a thin line followed by a thick line, is used at the end of a piece. Two thin lines next to each other mark the end of a section of a piece.

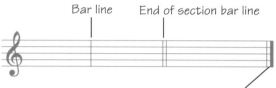

Bar line    End of section bar line

Double bar line

The number of beats in a measure affects the sound of the music. Normally, the first beat of a measure sounds slightly stronger than the others. Below you can see three versions of a tune with the bar lines in different places. Sing or play them, making the first beat in each measure the loudest, to hear how different the versions sound.

> **Can you write two sixteenth notes followed by an eighth note beamed together?**

## Time signatures

A **time signature** is a pair of numbers at the start of a piece of music which tell you how to count. The top number shows how many beats there are in each measure. The bottom number shows what type of beat they are: 4 means they are quarter beats, 8 means they are eighth beats, and 2 means they are half beats.

> **What do you think the time signatures $\frac{3}{2}$, $\frac{6}{4}$ and $\frac{12}{8}$ mean?**

$\frac{2}{4}$ 2 quarter beats in a measure

$\frac{3}{8}$ 3 eighth beats in a measure

$\frac{3}{4}$ 3 quarter beats in a measure

$\frac{6}{8}$ 6 eighth beats in a measure

$\frac{4}{4}$ or **C** 4 quarter beats in a measure

$\frac{2}{2}$ or **¢** 2 half beats in a measure

## Beaming

Eighth notes and shorter notes next to each other are often joined in groups by lines called **beams**. One beam means the notes are eighths, two means they are sixteenths, and so on. The groups fit the beats. Find out more on pages 20-21.

Sixteenth notes: two beams

Thirty-second notes: three beams

Eighth note and two sixteenth notes

## More about ties

A note which lasts too long to fit in a measure has to be written as two or more notes in different measures **tied** together.

These tied notes show one note lasting for eight quarter beats.

Sometimes, notes which last across different beats in a measure are written as two tied notes. This is to make it clear where each beat starts, so the rhythm is easier to count.

This note lasts for the first beat and part of the second beat.

## Debussy: *The girl with the flaxen hair* (for piano)

**Time signature.** Three quarter beats in a measure.

**Tied notes.** Means one note lasting for one and a half quarter beats.

**Beams.** These notes are joined by beams in a group lasting for one quarter beat.

**Tied notes** across a bar line. Means you play one note lasting for four quarter beats.

**Eighth notes** are joined by one **beam**.

**Legato** means "smooth".

**Sixteenth notes** are joined by two **beams**.

**Tied notes** across a bar line. Means you play one note lasting for two quarter beats.

## Whole measure rests

A rest which lasts for a whole measure can be written as a **whole rest** in any time signature except $\frac{4}{2}$. This avoids writing several rests to fill up the measure.

This rest lasts for three quarter beats.

This rest lasts for two quarter beats.

## Anacrusis

Some tunes start part of the way through a measure. This is known as an **anacrusis** or **upbeat**. When this happens, the last measure is also incomplete. The number of beats in the first and last measures add up to make one whole measure.

## Changing a time signature

The rhythms below sound similar because the pattern of long and short notes is the same. But the beats are quarters in the first rhythm and halfs in the second.

You can rewrite a tune in another time signature, so long as there are the same number of beats in a measure, and each note lasts for the same number of beats.

## Anon: *Greensleeves* (for voice)

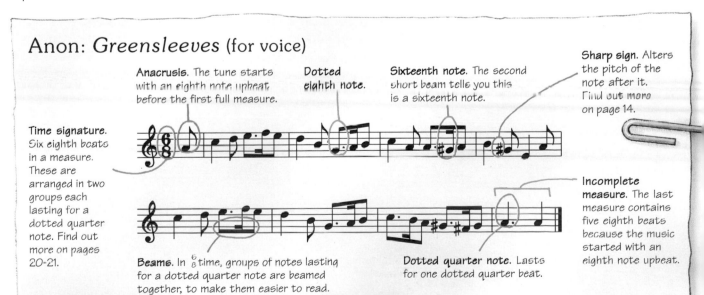

**Anacrusis.** The tune starts with an eighth note upbeat, before the first full measure.

**Dotted eighth note.**

**Sixteenth note.** The second short beam tells you this is a sixteenth note.

**Sharp sign.** Alters the pitch of the note after it. Find out more on page 14.

**Time signature.** Six eighth beats in a measure. These are arranged in two groups each lasting for a dotted quarter note. Find out more on pages 20-21.

**Beams.** In $\frac{6}{8}$ time, groups of notes lasting for a dotted quarter note are beamed together, to make them easier to read.

**Dotted quarter note.** Lasts for one dotted quarter beat.

**Incomplete measure.** The last measure contains five eighth beats because the music started with an eighth note upbeat.

# DIFFERENT WAYS OF WRITING MUSIC

The way music is written down is called notation. The system of notation used in most places today developed in Europe over hundreds of years. You can find out about early ways of writing music, and about some other notation systems, on these two pages.

This decorated letter shows someone playing a small organ. It comes from a 15th-century music manuscript.

## Early notation

A thousand years ago, people drew dots, lines and curves in songbooks to show roughly where the tune got higher or lower. These signs, called neumes, did not show the exact pitch of each note.

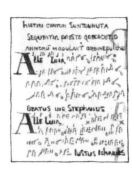

An early song manuscript with neumes

At the beginning of the 11th century, an Italian called Guido of Arezzo began to develop the use of horizontal lines to show the pitch of notes. He also used a drawing known as the Guidonian hand, with short words and notes written on it, to help teach people how to sing from written music.

The Guidonian hand

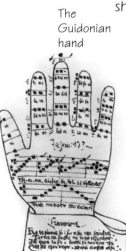

At first, notes were written as solid diamonds or rectangles. The way they were spaced out gave musicians clues about how long each one lasted.

Below you can see a late 13th-century manuscript of a song called Sumer is icumen in.

Music was often beautifully decorated with drawings. Occasionally, composers even wrote pieces in shapes.

This is a late 14th-century or early 15th-century love song in the shape of a heart by Baude Cordier.

Gradually, composers began to use open noteheads and dots to indicate exactly how long each note should last.

The songs in this 15th-century collection show precise note lengths.

Oval noteheads eventually replaced diamond-shaped and rectangular ones. During the 16th and 17th centuries, composers began to follow a standard system of bar lines, beams, slurs and clefs.

## Writing ornaments

Even after a standard system of notation developed, composers used many different symbols to indicate ornaments (extra decorative notes). Sometimes they published charts to explain how to play them. Today it can be difficult to know exactly what some of the different symbols mean.

Jean-Philippe Rameau published this chart, showing how to play ornaments, in a book of harpsichord music.

## Tablature

Tablature is an old system of notation which is still often used today for guitar music. Modern guitar tablature uses sets of six lines, one for each string on the guitar. Numbers on the lines tell the player exactly where to press the strings.

This song by John Dowland from the late 1500s has the lute part in tablature on the left page. It is written so the musicians can stand around it.

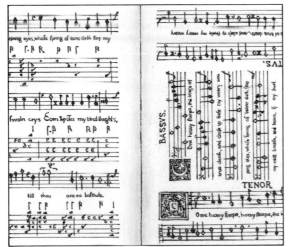

## Aleatory music

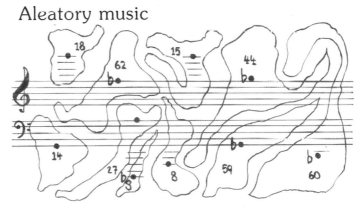

Part of *Concert for Piano and Orchestra* by John Cage, one of the main composers of aleatory music

Aleatory music is a type of music which developed in the 20th century. It allows each performer to decide exactly how to play the music. For example, you might have to choose which notes to use, how long to make them, or what order to play different sections in. It is often written using elements of standard notation combined with shapes, lines or patterns.

## Other types of notation

In some parts of the world, other notation systems developed.

This 13th-century Arabic manuscript shows notes and rhythms as letters and numbers.

This 16th-century song manuscript is from Japan. Signs next to the words show how to sing them.

This is part of an elaborately decorated 15th-century music manuscript.

# SHARPS, FLATS AND NATURALS

Sharps, flats and naturals are signs which alter the pitch of notes. When they are used during a piece they are called **accidentals**. They can also appear at the beginning of a staff (see pages 18-19).

| # | ♭ | ♮ |
|---|---|---|
| Sharp | Flat | Natural |

The first pianos, known as fortepianos, were much quieter than modern pianos (see page 32). The one above was specially made for Beethoven.

## Tones and semitones

The distance in pitch between two notes is called an **interval**. The smallest interval on a piano is called a **semitone**. An interval equal to two semitones is called a **tone**. The diagram of a keyboard below shows some pairs of keys which play notes a semitone or a tone apart.

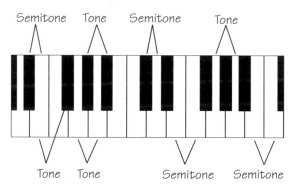

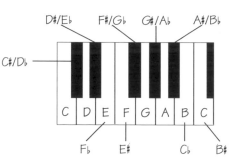

The note F sharp on a piano or keyboard sounds exactly the same as G flat, because they are played with the same key. Two notes with the same sound but different names are called **enharmonics**. You can find out about when to use different enharmonic versions of a note on page 17. Each pair of notes below sounds the same on a piano.

## Sharps, flats and naturals

A **sharp** sign (#) raises the pitch of a note by a semitone. For example, F sharp (F#) is a semitone higher than F. A **flat** sign (♭) lowers the pitch of a note by a semitone. For example, B flat (B♭) is a semitone lower than B. Sharp or flat signs are placed in front of the notes they apply to, on the same line or space. A note which is not a sharp or flat is called a **natural**.

F# = G♭   A# = B♭   E# = F   B = C♭

On most instruments, except the piano or keyboard, the player can control the pitch to a fraction of a semitone, so F sharp may be slightly higher than G flat.

F sharp          B flat

The keys on a piano are named after the notes they play. A black key plays the sharp note of the white key directly on its left. It also plays the flat note of the white key directly on its right. So each black key has two names. Pairs of white keys with no black keys between them have two names too: each plays the sharp or flat version of the other.

## How accidentals work

An accidental during a piece affects all the notes on that line or space which follow it in the measure. The bar line cancels the accidental. To cancel a sharp or flat before the end of a measure, a natural sign (♮) is used. This then affects any notes on that line or space following it in the measure.

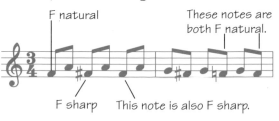

F natural

These notes are both F natural.

F sharp   This note is also F sharp.

Beethoven scribbled tiny fragments of musical ideas in his notebooks.

# Beethoven: *Bagatelle* (for piano)

**Piano system.** Consists of two staves joined by a curly bracket. The top staff is played with the right hand and the bottom staff with the left hand. The first system usually starts a little to the right of the other systems.

**Chord.** Two or more notes played at the same time (see pages 34-37).

**B flat.** Accidentals only apply to the staff they are written on. This note needs a flat sign even though there is a B flat on the lower staff earlier in the measure.

**B natural.** Sometimes a natural sign is used at the beginning of a measure when there has just been a flat or sharp version of the same note. It reminds the player that the bar line has canceled the accidental.

**B flat.**

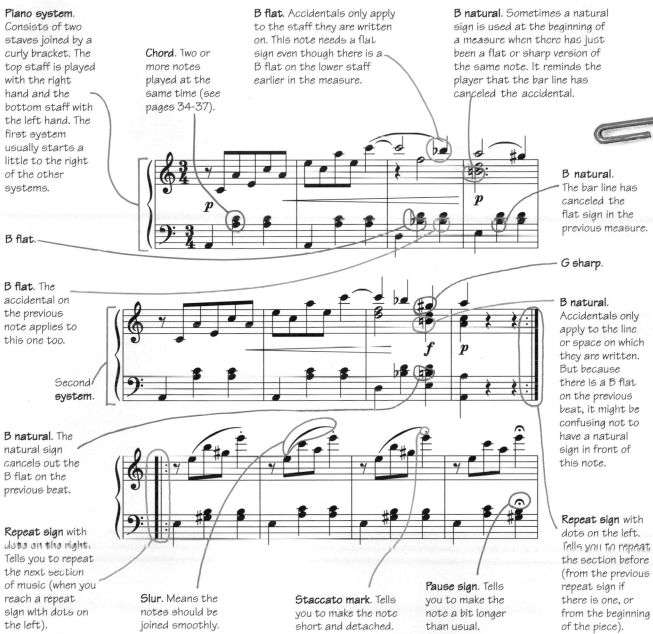

**B natural.** The bar line has canceled the flat sign in the previous measure.

**G sharp.**

**B flat.** The accidental on the previous note applies to this one too.

**Second system.**

**B natural.** Accidentals only apply to the line or space on which they are written. But because there is a B flat on the previous beat, it might be confusing not to have a natural sign in front of this note.

**B natural.** The natural sign cancels out the B flat on the previous beat.

**Repeat sign** with dots on the right. Tells you to repeat the next section of music (when you reach a repeat sign with dots on the left).

**Slur.** Means the notes should be joined smoothly.

**Staccato mark.** Tells you to make the note short and detached.

**Pause sign.** Tells you to make the note a bit longer than usual.

**Repeat sign** with dots on the left. Tells you to repeat the section before (from the previous repeat sign if there is one, or from the beginning of the piece).

## Double sharps and flats

**Double sharps** (×) and **double flats** (♭♭) raise or lower a note by two semitones (one tone). They are used like other accidentals, and affect notes which follow in the measure on that line or space.

They can be canceled during a measure by another accidental on that line or space.

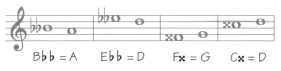

Bbb = A    Ebb = D    Fx = G    Cx = D

# SCALES

Most music is based on scales. A **scale** is a sequence of notes going up or down in which the intervals between the notes follow a fixed pattern. There are lots of different kinds of scales. The type of scale used affects the sound of the music.

This is the type of dance on which Dvořák based his *Slavonic dances*.

## Major scales

One of the most common types of scales is the **major scale**. It contains two types of intervals: tones and semitones (see page 14). On the way up (**ascending**), they come in this order: tone - tone - semitone - tone - tone - tone - semitone.

C major scale          T=tone   S=semitone

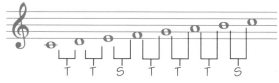

Major scales have the same notes going down (**descending**) as ascending, so the order of the intervals is reversed.

Major scales are named after the note they start on (the **tonic** or **keynote**). The scale above is a C major scale. It is the only major scale which has no sharps or flats. A major scale starting on any other note has to include at least one sharp or flat in order to preserve the correct sequence of intervals. For example, the scale of G major includes F sharp. The scale of F major includes B flat.

G major scale        This note has to be F sharp to make it a tone above E.

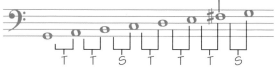

F major scale        This note has to be B flat to make it a semitone above A.

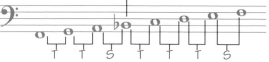

Can you write out major and minor scales starting on D below Middle C, using the bass clef?

## Minor scales

There are two types of **minor scale**: harmonic (often learned first) and melodic. The sequence of intervals for a melodic minor scale varies depending on whether it is ascending or descending.

C melodic minor scale. On the way up, the third note is a semitone lower than in the major scale.

On the way down, the two notes after the tonic are also a semitone lower than in the major scale.

C harmonic minor scale. The third and sixth notes are a semitone lower than in the major scale, on the way up and down.

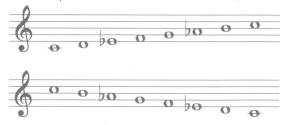

Melodic minor scales are normally used for writing tunes, and harmonic minor scales for writing chords.

There is a chart of major and minor scales on pages 42-43.

## Arpeggios

A major or minor **arpeggio** consists of the tonic, third and fifth notes of a major or minor scale.

G major arpeggio          G minor arpeggio

## Using the correct enharmonic

Major and minor scales always use one note with each letter name. This means when you need to use a sharp or flat, you use the enharmonic version with a different letter name from the other notes in the scale.

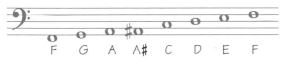

F  G  A  A#  C  D  E  F

This F major scale is wrong, because there is no note with the name B. The A# should be B♭.

## Names for notes in a scale

There is a special name for each note in a major or minor scale. The **tonic** is the note at the beginning and end. The next most important note is the fifth note, which is called the **dominant**.

Tonic   Mediant   Dominant   Leading note

Supertonic   Sub-dominant   Sub-mediant   Tonic

Schoenberg developed a system of writing music called serialism, based on chromatic scales (see below).

---

## Dvořák: *Slavonic dance* (for piano duet or orchestra)

G minor scales have **B flats** instead of Bs.

The first four measures are based on the scale of **G melodic minor**.

The second four measures are based on the scale of **G major**.

The Bs are **naturals** in a G major scale.

**Spread chord.** The notes are played quickly one after the other, starting with the lowest, then held to the end of the chord.

The first four measures sound solemn and heavy because they are based on a minor scale.

The second four measures sound much brighter because they are based on a major scale.

---

## Other types of scales

**Chromatic scales** are often used in 20th-century music. Each interval is a semitone. A chromatic scale can be written using different enharmonics. But each letter name should appear at least once, and not more than twice in a row.

The scales below are both correct versions of a chromatic scale starting on D.

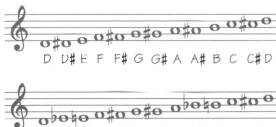

D  D#  E  F  F#  G  G#  A  A#  B  C  C#  D

D  E♭  E♮  F  F#  G  G#  A  B♭  B♮  C  C#  D

A **pentatonic scale** consists of five notes, followed by the note an octave apart from the first note. A lot of folk music from Europe, as well as traditional music from China, Japan, Indonesia and parts of Africa, is based on pentatonic scales.

Pentatonic scale

Some 20th-century music uses **whole tone scales**. In these scales, each interval is a tone. There are no semitones.

Whole tone scale

Debussy often used whole tone scales in his music.

# KEYS AND KEY SIGNATURES

Music based on a major or minor scale is said to be in a **key**. **Key signatures** are used to tell you which sharps and flats are used in this key. They apply throughout a piece.

Can you write out major and minor scales starting on D below Middle C, using the bass clef, with the correct key signatures?

## Key signatures

A **key signature** is the name given to one or more sharps or flats next to the clef. It applies to any notes with the same letter name as a line or space on which the signs are written. This effect can be canceled by an accidental during the piece. You write a key signature on each staff of a piece. This saves writing out lots of accidentals.

*One sharp in the key signature on the F line: all the Fs are F sharps*

*One flat in the key signature on the B line: all the Bs are B flats*

Each key signature contains either sharps or flats, never both. The number of sharps or flats depends on the scale on which the music is based. For example, a piece based on a C major scale has no key signature, because the scale has no sharps or flats. A piece based on a G major scale has one sharp in the key signature: F sharp.

For pieces based on minor scales, the key signature contains the sharps or flats in the descending melodic minor scale. For example, a piece based on a C melodic minor scale has a key signature of three flats, B flat, E flat and A flat.

*C melodic minor scale, descending*

Bb    Ab        Eb

## Keys

Music is said to be in the **key** of the scale it is based on. A piece based on a C major scale is said to be in the key of C major (or C). Music based on a G melodic minor scale is in the key of G minor.

## The order of sharps and flats

If you know how many sharps or flats there are in a particular key signature, you can work out which ones they are. This is because the sharps and flats always come in a particular order. For sharps the order is F, C, G, D, A, E, B. So a key signature with four sharps will contain the first four sharps in the list: F, C, G and D. Flats come in this order: B, E, A, D, G, C, F. A key signature with three flats will contain the first three flats in the list: B, E and A.

The sharps or flats have to be written in a certain way on the staff.

*These key signatures show which lines and spaces to write the sharp and flat signs on.*

## Figuring out a key signature

It is easy to figure out how many sharps there are in a major key. The seventh note of the ascending major scale (the leading note), which is a semitone below the tonic, is always the last sharp in that key. In an A major scale, the seventh note is G sharp, a semitone below A. So the key of A major contains all the sharps in the list up to and including G sharp. This means the key of A major has three sharps: F, C and G.

For major keys containing flats, the fourth note of the ascending scale (the sub-dominant) is the last flat in that key. The fourth note of an F major scale is B flat. Since this is the first flat in the list, it is the only one in the key of F major.

To figure out the key of a piece, look at which sharps and flats it contains, whether it sounds major or minor, and which note it ends on (usually the tonic).

Try to think up sentences in which the words start with the names of the sharps or flats, in the correct order. (This will help you remember them.)

The picture above shows a catalog in which Haydn listed many of his pieces.

## Mozart: *Concerto in E flat* (for horn and orchestra)

**Key signature** of E flat major has three flats (the last is A flat, the fourth note of an E flat major scale).

**B flat.**

**E flat.**

This is **B flat** too, even though it is written in a different octave.

**A flat.**

**Acciaccatura.** Played very quickly before the beat. Find out more on page 38.

**Key signature** appears on each staff of a piece.

**E flat.** The flat in the key signature applies to Es in any octave.

## Relative major and minor keys

A major and minor key are said to be **relative** if they have the same key signature. Each major and minor key has a relative minor or major.

The sixth note (or sub-mediant) of a major scale is the tonic of the relative minor. For example, the sixth note of a C major scale is A. So A minor is the relative minor. Both C major and A minor have no sharps or flats in the key signature. (A descending melodic minor scale starting on A has no sharps or flats.)

You can figure this out in reverse, too. The sixth note going down the scale of A melodic minor is C. This is the tonic of the relative major key (C major).

You can look up which major and minor keys are relative on pages 42-43.

## How different keys sound

Playing a piece in a different key from the one in which it was written is called **transposing**. Although the intervals between the notes stay exactly the same in a different key, the music may have a different mood. It might sound bright in one key, but darker and more mysterious in another.

The first few measures of the Mozart piece above, in the keys of F major and C major

In Mozart's time, musicians had to insert or remove sections of their horn to play in different keys.

## Haydn: *Gypsy dance* (for piano)

**Key signature** has three flats: B flat, E flat and A flat. Could be the key of E flat major, or the relative minor, which is C minor.

The scale of C melodic minor contains a B natural. So this tune is in the key of C minor.

The music has a minor sound.

**B natural.** Not consistent with the key of E flat major.

Tune ends on C, not E flat.

# GROUPING NOTES AND RESTS

Notes and rests in a measure are arranged in groups, to make the rhythm easy to read. In some time signatures (called **simple time**), the groups are based on the type of beat shown by the bottom number in the time signature. But in others (called **compound time**) they are based on longer beats.

## Simple time

The chart below shows the type of beat used for grouping notes in simple time signatures, and the number of these beats in each measure.

Above you can see a scene from Rossini's *The barber of Seville.*

|  | 2 beats in a measure (**double time**) | 3 beats in a measure (**triple time**) | 4 beats in a measure (**quadruple time**) |
|---|---|---|---|
| Quarter beats | $\frac{2}{4}$ | $\frac{3}{4}$ | $\frac{4}{4}$ |
| Half beats | $\frac{2}{2}$ | $\frac{3}{2}$ | $\frac{4}{2}$ |
| Eighth beats | $\frac{2}{8}$ | $\frac{3}{8}$ | $\frac{4}{8}$ |

## Rules for grouping in simple time

1. Try to use dotted notes instead of ties.
2. In $\frac{2}{4}$ and $\frac{3}{4}$ you can beam a whole measure of eighth notes. In $\frac{4}{4}$, you can beam up to four eighth notes together.
3. In quadruple time (such as $\frac{4}{4}$), don't write a beam or rest across the second and third beats of a measure.
4. Beam sixteenth notes and shorter notes together in beats.
5. Write a whole rest for a whole measure's silence, except in $\frac{4}{2}$. In quadruple time, you can write a two-beat rest for the first or last two beats in a measure. In other cases, write a new rest for each beat of a silence, but don't use more rests than you need.

**Rossini: *The barber of Seville* (opera overture)**

These rests are not written as a half rest, because it would go across the second and third beats of the measure (**rule 3**).

Half rest on first two beats of measure (**rule 5**).

**Staccato mark.** Means the note is short and detached.

Three eighth notes beamed together (**rule 2**).

This eighth note is not joined to the next pair, because the beam would go across the second and third beats of the measure (**rule 3**).

In $\frac{3}{4}$, three eighth notes after a dotted quarter note are not usually beamed together. This is because the measure might look as though it is in $\frac{6}{8}$ (see page 21).

**Parry: *Jerusalem* (hymn)**

This is written as a dotted note, not two tied notes (**rule 1**).

Notes are beamed in quarter beats.

## Triplets

Three equal notes played in the time of two are called **triplets**. For example, three triplet eighth notes last for the same time as two normal eighth notes, or one quarter beat. Triplets are shown by a *3*.

This group adds up to three eighth notes. The triplet sign tells you it lasts for one quarter beat.

## Compound time

This chart shows the type of beat used for grouping notes in compound time signatures, and the number of these beats in a measure.

|  | 2 beats in a measure (double time) | 3 beats in a measure (triple time) | 4 beats in a measure (quadruple time) |
|---|---|---|---|
| Dotted quarter beats | $\frac{6}{8}$ | $\frac{9}{8}$ | $\frac{12}{8}$ |
| Dotted half beats | $\frac{6}{4}$ | $\frac{9}{4}$ | $\frac{12}{4}$ |
| Dotted eighth beats | $\frac{6}{16}$ | $\frac{9}{16}$ | $\frac{12}{16}$ |

## Grouping in compound time

1. Write a one-beat, two-beat or four-beat note as a single dotted note.
2. Write a three-beat note as a two-beat note tied to a one-beat note.
3. For a note which does not last for a whole number of beats, but goes across two beats in a measure, write two tied notes. This helps to make it clear how the rhythm fits the beats.
4. Beam eighth notes and shorter notes together in beats.
5. You can write a one-beat rest as one dotted rest, or as two rests, with the longer one first. For a rest lasting for the last two-thirds of a beat, you write two rests not one. In other cases, follow the rules for writing rests in simple time (see rule 5 on page 20).

Grieg was very interested in traditional Norwegian music. The tune below comes from a piece to accompany a play by the Norwegian writer Ibsen.

**Grieg: *Morning* (from *Peer Gynt*, for orchestra)**

Notes beamed in dotted quarter beats (**rule 4**).

Two tied notes instead of a half note because the note goes across two beats (**rule 3**).

**Mozart: *Concerto in B flat* (for piano and orchestra)**

A beam can continue across a rest within a group of notes, to make each beat clear.

Dotted quarter beat.

Two eighth rests, not a quarter rest, for the last two-thirds of the beat (**rule 5**).

## Duplets and other divisions

Two equal notes played in the time of three are called **duplets** (shown by a *2*). A beat can also be divided into other numbers of equal notes.

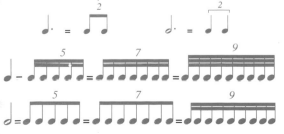

## Other time signatures

In some time signatures, such as $\frac{5}{4}$ or $\frac{7}{4}$, the beats divide into unequal groups. The order of these groups can vary.

In $\frac{5}{4}$ or $\frac{5}{8}$, each measure divides into a two-beat group and a three-beat group.

In $\frac{7}{4}$ or $\frac{7}{8}$, each measure divides into a three-beat group and two two-beat groups.

Look at the music extracts throughout this book to see other examples of how notes and rests are grouped.

# MUSIC THROUGH THE AGES

Musical styles and fashions in Europe have been changing over hundreds of years. Here you can find out about some of the most important developments.

This instrument, called a hurdy-gurdy, was popular with traveling musicians.

## Early music

Over a thousand years ago, monks in Christian churches sang a type of music called plainchant, in which they all sang the same tune together. Gradually, they began to sing different tunes at the same time. This style, known as polyphony, was used for hundreds of years.

Monks singing

Musicians accompanying an acrobat

Small bands of traveling musicians made a living by singing at village dances or fairs and at noblemen's feasts. They sang and played instruments, and often juggled or performed acrobatics too.

The lute was a very important instrument in Renaissance music. It was often used for accompanying songs and for solo playing.

## Renaissance music

Music written in the 15th and 16th centuries is often called Renaissance music. During this time, triads (see page 34) became the basis of music. Music was a very important part of education, and many people played music or sang with their friends.

This early 16th-century painting shows a singer accompanied by a flute and a lute.

In the late 16th century, a type of song called a madrigal was very popular. Madrigals were for a few people, each singing a different line of music.

This painting shows people singing a madrigal.

## Baroque music

In the Baroque period (the 17th and early 18th centuries), the use of chords (see pages 34-37) was developed. One of the most popular types of music was the suite, which was a collection of dance music.

Suites often included a minuet.

The first operas (plays set to music) were written in Italy in the early 17th century, and were usually about heroes in history or legend. They often used spectacular scenery and special effects.

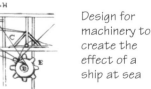

Design for machinery to create the effect of a ship at sea

At around the same time, ballet began to develop in France, and operas often contained ballet dancing.

## Classical music

The Classical period lasted from the late 18th century to the early 19th century. Composers tried to make their music balanced and graceful. Many types of music, such as symphonies (for orchestra), concertos (for soloist and orchestra) and sonatas (for soloist, often with piano accompaniment) became standard during this time.

Vienna, in Austria, was an important musical center in the Classical period.

A group of instruments called a string quartet, consisting of two violins, a viola and a cello became very popular.

A silhouette of a string quartet from around 1750

## Romantic music

In the 19th century, many composers thought that feeling and imagination should be the basis of music. This period was known as the Romantic period. Many composers were also inspired by the traditional music of their own countries. Some of the most famous operas and ballets were written at this time.

A scene from *The Nutcracker*, a ballet by Pyotr Il'yich Tchaikovsky

## Music in the 20th century

In the 20th century, ways of recording music and altering sounds electronically have enabled composers to experiment with many new sounds. New systems for writing music have also been invented, including whole tone scales and serialism (see page 17).

Many other types of music, including ragtime, blues, jazz and pop, have developed. Often, these combine ideas from past styles, as well as from other musical styles around the world.

The ballet *Elite Syncopations* is based on ragtime music by Scott Joplin.

## When composers lived

Below you can find out the dates of all the composers whose music appears in this book (c. means "around").

Thomas Tallis (c.1505-1585)
Thomas Morley (c.1557-1602)
Archangelo Corelli
    (1653-1713)
Henry Purcell (1659-1695)
Antonio Vivaldi (1678-1741)
Georg Philipp Telemann
    (1681-1767)
Jean-Philippe Rameau
    (1683-1764)

Johann Sebastian Bach
    (1685-1750)
George Frideric Handel
    (1685-1759)
Joseph Haydn (1732-1809)
Wolfgang Amadeus Mozart
    (1756-1791)
Ludwig van Beethoven
    (1770-1827)
Fernando Sor (1778-1839)
Gioachino Rossini
    (1792-1868)
Franz Schubert (1797-1828)
Felix Mendelssohn
    (1809-1847)

Robert Schumann (1810-1856)
Fryderyk Chopin (1810-1849)
Charles Gounod (1818-1893)
Johannes Brahms (1833-1897)
Camille Saint-Saëns
    (1835-1921)
Pyotr Il'yich Tchaikovsky
    (1840-1893)
Antonín Dvořák (1841-1904)
Edvard Grieg (1843-1907)
Nikolay Rimsky-Korsakov
    (1844-1908)
Gabriel Fauré (1845-1924)
Hubert Parry (1848-1918)
Claude Debussy (1862-1918)

# INTERVALS

Schumann wrote some of his piano music for his wife, Clara, who was a famous pianist.

If two notes are played together, the interval between them is called **harmonic**, and if they are played one after the other, it is called **melodic**. Intervals which can be found in a major or minor scale starting on the lower note are known as **diatonic**. Other intervals are known as **chromatic**.

## Calculating an interval

When you calculate an interval, you always start from the lower of the two notes. Counting this note as one, you count up the lines and spaces until you reach the upper note. This gives you the number of each interval.

2nd  3rd  4th  5th  6th  7th  Octave

But the number of the interval alone is not enough to identify it. This is because if you add an accidental to one of these notes, the interval changes, but the number will stay the same.

These intervals are all types of 5th.

The words **major**, **minor**, **perfect**, **augmented** and **diminished** are used to distinguish between different types of intervals with the same number.

Which notes are a minor 7th, an augmented 4th, and a perfect 12th above the note G?

## Diatonic intervals

Intervals between the tonic and other notes in a major scale are named major or perfect, depending on the interval.

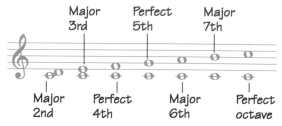

Major 3rd   Perfect 5th   Major 7th

Major 2nd   Perfect 4th   Major 6th   Perfect octave

In a minor scale, most of these intervals stay the same. There are three new ones.

Minor 3rd   Minor 6th   Minor 7th

Each interval shown below appears in a major or minor scale which starts on the lower note.

Perfect 4th   Major 2nd   Minor 7th   Major 6th   Minor 3rd   Perfect 5th

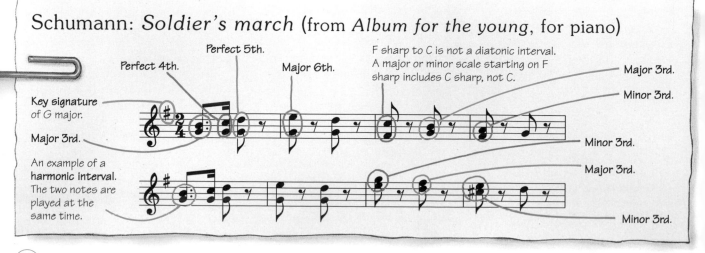

## Schumann: *Soldier's march* (from *Album for the young*, for piano)

Perfect 4th.

Perfect 5th.

Major 6th.

F sharp to C is not a diatonic interval. A major or minor scale starting on F sharp includes C sharp, not C.

Major 3rd.

Minor 3rd.

Key signature of G major.

Major 3rd.

An example of a harmonic interval. The two notes are played at the same time.

Minor 3rd.

Major 3rd.

Minor 3rd.

## Chromatic intervals

Chromatic intervals include minor seconds, and diminished and augmented intervals. An **augmented** interval is a semitone bigger than a perfect or major one. A **diminished** interval is a semitone smaller than a perfect or minor one. A **minor** interval is a semitone smaller than a major one. A **perfect** interval has no major or minor version.

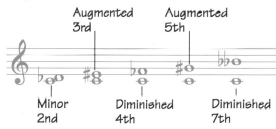

## Different names

Some intervals with different names sound the same. This is because they use different enharmonic versions of the same note.

These two intervals sound the same.

Augmented 3rd    Perfect 4th

## Compound intervals

An interval greater than an octave is called **compound**. Count up the lines and spaces to find the number.

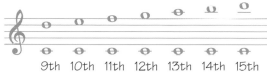

9th  10th  11th  12th  13th  14th  15th

The rest of the name is the same as if the upper note were an octave lower.

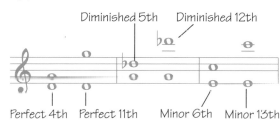

The rest of the name is the same as if the upper note were an octave lower.

Alternatively, you can name the interval as if the upper note were an octave lower, but using the word compound.

Compound perfect 4th    Compound diminished 5th    Compound minor 6th

Tchaikovsky rewrote the piece below several times, in order to please a music critic.

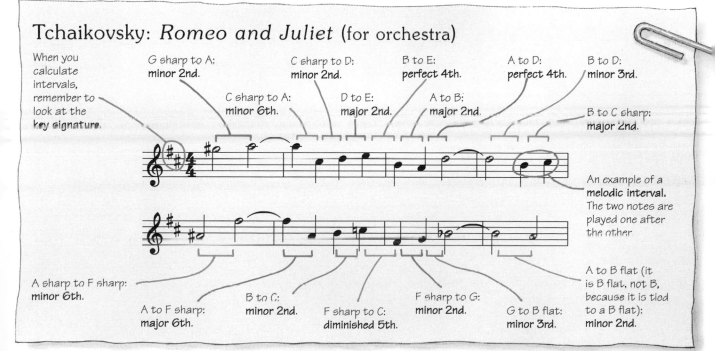

# Tchaikovsky: *Romeo and Juliet* (for orchestra)

When you calculate intervals, remember to look at the key signature.

G sharp to A: minor 2nd.

C sharp to A: minor 6th.

C sharp to D: minor 2nd.

D to E: major 2nd.

B to E: perfect 4th.

A to B: major 2nd.

A to D: perfect 4th.

B to D: minor 3rd.

B to C sharp: major 2nd.

An example of a melodic interval. The two notes are played one after the other.

A sharp to F sharp: minor 6th.

A to F sharp: major 6th.

B to C: minor 2nd.

F sharp to C: diminished 5th.

F sharp to G: minor 2nd.

G to B flat: minor 3rd.

A to B flat (it is B flat, not B, because it is tied to a B flat): minor 2nd.

# TRANSPOSING

Rewriting music at a different pitch is called **transposing**. This can be very useful, for example if you want to play something higher or lower than written, or in a different clef. Some instruments, known as **transposing instruments**, play at a different pitch from the written notes.

The guitar is a transposing instrument which sounds notes an octave lower than they are written.

The piccolo is a transposing instrument which sounds notes an octave higher than they are written.

## Transposing by an octave

Transposing music up or down by an octave is fairly easy. Each new note has the same name as before, and the key signature and accidentals stay the same. Below you can see a tune transposed up an octave.

The tune starts on the G above Middle C.

This is the tune transposed up an octave.

You can transpose music up or down an octave and rewrite it in another clef too. This is particularly useful if you want to play music written in the wrong clef for your instrument. Below you can see the original tune transposed down an octave and written in different clefs.

The tune now starts on the G below Middle C, an octave lower than in the original version.

## Transposing by other intervals

Sometimes you might want to transpose music by a smaller interval, perhaps to make it easier to sing or play. When you do this, the key of the music changes. To find the new tonic, you transpose the original tonic by the same interval as the other notes. Then you can work out what the new key signature is (see pages 18-19 and 42-43).

Can you rewrite the clarinet part of the piece by Beethoven on page 27 at the pitch it sounds?

This tune is in the key of F major.

If the tune is transposed up a major 3rd it will be in the key of A major (A is a major 3rd above F).

If the tune is transposed up a perfect 5th it will be in the key of C major (C is a perfect 5th above F).

If the original music has any accidentals, watch out carefully for these when you transpose it. You will need accidentals in all the same places, but they may be different from the ones in the original. Look at what happens to the accidental in the tune below when it is transposed into different keys.

This tune is in A minor. The sharp sign in measure 1 raises the G by a semitone.

In C minor (transposed up a minor 3rd), there is a B flat in the key signature, so the B in measure 1 needs a natural to raise it by a semitone.

In B minor (transposed up a major 2nd), the A in measure 1 needs a sharp to raise it by a semitone.

# Transposing instruments

Some wind instruments come in different sizes, each of which plays at a different pitch. To make it easier for players to change from one to another, each written note is played with the same fingering on each instrument, but sounds a different pitch. The instruments are named after the note that sounds when they play a written C. For example, the type of clarinet which sounds a written C as B flat is called a clarinet in B flat. In a piece for clarinet and piano, the clarinet and piano parts are written in different keys so they sound the same.

## Beethoven: *Quintet in E flat*
### (for piano, oboe, clarinet, horn and bassoon)

All the instruments are in **unison** (playing the same notes at the same time) in this extract.

Music for the **clarinet in B flat** is written a major second above the notes it sounds. The key is a major second above the key of the piano part: F major, not E flat major.

The **oboe** is not a transposing instrument, so its music is in E flat major, the same key as the piano part.

**Double dotted eighth note.** Lasts for an eighth plus half an eighth (a sixteenth) plus quarter of an eighth (a thirty-second).

**Sixty-fourth note.** Lasts for half a thirty-second (there are sixteen in one quarter beat). It has four tails or beams.

This written note C sounds as B flat, a major second lower.

Music for the **horn in E flat** is written a major sixth above the notes it sounds. The key is a major sixth above the key of the piano part: C major, not E flat major.

This written note C sounds as E flat, a major sixth lower.

The **bassoon** is not a transposing instrument, so its music is in E flat major, the same key as the piano part.

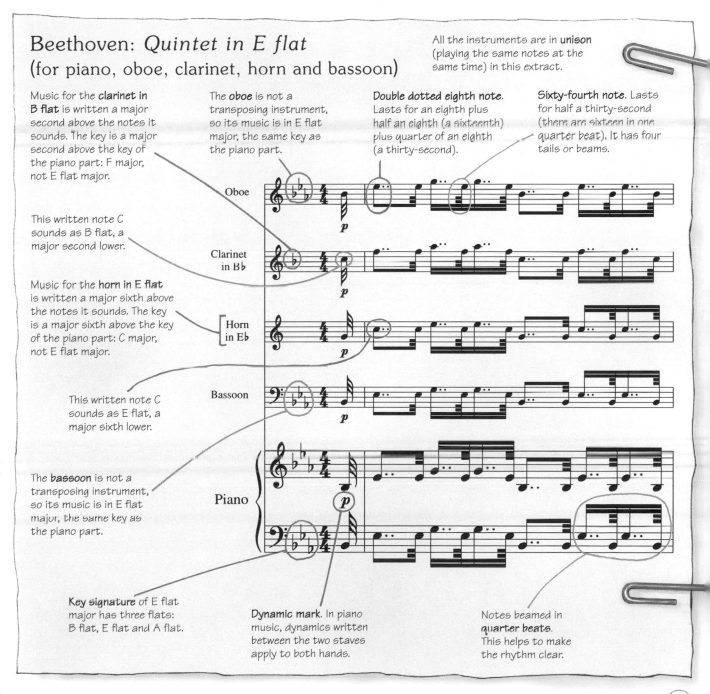

Key signature of E flat major has three flats: B flat, E flat and A flat.

**Dynamic mark.** In piano music, dynamics written between the two staves apply to both hands.

Notes beamed in **quarter beats**. This helps to make the rhythm clear.

27

# PHRASES

For a tune to make sense, it needs a structure, just as writing needs sentences and punctuation. Tunes are built from groups of notes which sound as though they belong together as an idea. These groups are known as **phrases**, and are usually separated by a tiny silence when the music is sung or played.

This is the title page of a score of *Scheherazade* by Rimsky-Korsakov.

## Identifying phrases

Musicians often disagree about where phrases start and finish. This is because there is often more than one possible **interpretation**. When you play music, try to hear which notes belong together. Phrases may be the same length, or start on the same beat of a measure. Songs may have a phrase for each line of words.

## Answering phrases

In some music, pairs of phrases of the same length sometimes seem to match each other. The first phrase seems to ask a question, and the second phrase to answer it. For example, the second phrase may seem to answer the first by ending on the tonic when the first phrase did not.

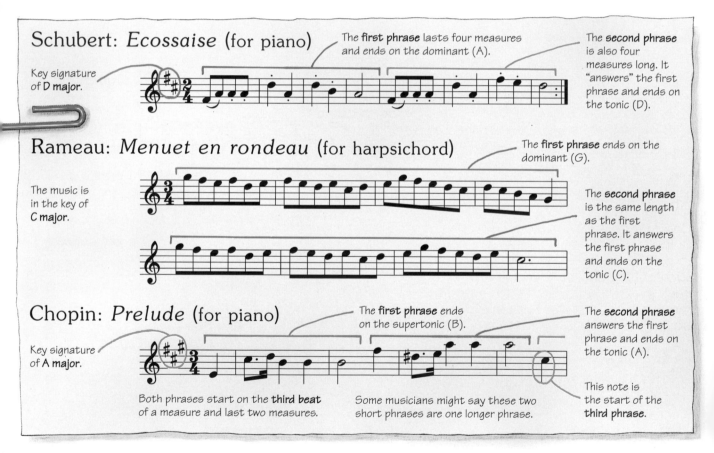

Schubert: *Ecossaise* (for piano)

Key signature of D major.

The **first phrase** lasts four measures and ends on the dominant (A).

The **second phrase** is also four measures long. It "answers" the first phrase and ends on the tonic (D).

Rameau: *Menuet en rondeau* (for harpsichord)

The music is in the key of C major.

The **first phrase** ends on the dominant (G).

The **second phrase** is the same length as the first phrase. It answers the first phrase and ends on the tonic (C).

Chopin: *Prelude* (for piano)

Key signature of A major.

The **first phrase** ends on the supertonic (B).

The **second phrase** answers the first phrase and ends on the tonic (A).

This note is the start of the **third phrase**.

Both phrases start on the **third beat** of a measure and last two measures.

Some musicians might say these two short phrases are one longer phrase.

## Rhythmic patterns

Phrases often have a strong rhythm structure. A pattern may be repeated or varied within a phrase, between phrases, or even throughout a whole piece.

## Melodic patterns

Phrases often contain patterns of notes which are repeated exactly, or changed by transposing them to a different pitch or varying the intervals.

## Grieg: *Piano concerto* (for piano and orchestra)

First phrase.

Tenuto mark. Tells you to hold the note for its full length, or even a little longer.

Second phrase.

Both phrases have exactly the same rhythm.

The notes are different in the second phrase, but they go up and down in the same pattern.

## Mozart: *Symphony no.40* (for orchestra)

The rhythm is the same in each phrase. The melody follows the same pattern in the first and third phrases, and in the second and fourth phrases.

First phrase.

Second phrase.

Beginning of **third phrase**.

**Fourth phrase.**

Each phrase starts on the **third beat** of a measure.

## Rimsky-Korsakov: *Scheherazade* (for orchestra)

First phrase.

Beginning of **second phrase**.

The melody of the second phrase sounds similar to the first, but more decorative.

This eighth note is not beamed to the next pair, to show it is in a different phrase.

## Showing phrases

Composers usually do not show phrases in their music. Instead, they show how to play notes within phrases, using signs such as **slurs** and **staccatos**. It is up to each player to decide how to phrase the music. Signs such as **breath marks** or **bowing** can help them do this.

## Phrases that modulate

Sometimes a phrase may end in a different key from the one it began in, such as the relative minor or major key. This is called **modulation**. For a tune to modulate clearly, it has to use a note which is in the scale of the new key but not in the scale of the original key.

## Morley: *Now is the month of maying* (song)

The first phrase starts in G major and modulates to D major.

The note C sharp is not in the key of G major.

D is the new tonic.

The breath mark suggests that a phrase has finished.

The second phrase modulates back to G major. The Cs are no longer C sharps.

# WORDS AND MUSIC

This manuscript in Purcell's handwriting is from a piece for choir. Purcell also wrote around two hundred songs.

Words which are set to music are known as **lyrics**. When composers write songs, they can use the rhythm and shape of the melody to help bring out the meaning and mood of the lyrics.

## Word rhythms

When you speak, words have a rhythm of their own. For example, one **syllable** (separate sound) may be stressed more than the others. In a sentence, short or unimportant words may be faster than longer or important ones. The meaning may also depend on which word you stress. For example, "Can I go?" has a slightly different meaning depending on whether you stress the word "I" or "go".

In a song, stressed syllables usually come on strong beats in the measure, for example the first beat. Important words often last longer than others.

$\frac{3}{4}$ ♩ ♩ ♩ | Stress on "I"     $\frac{3}{4}$ ♩ ♩ ♩. | Stress on "go"

The rhythms can fit the mood of the lyrics too, for example by being lively or gentle, smooth or spiky.

## Song melodies

Words can also be emphasized by the melody. For example, an important word may come on the highest note of a phrase, or last for several notes.

The word "I" is stressed.

The melody can also help to express the mood of the lyrics, for example by being major or minor, high or low.

## Writing lyrics with music

When you write out lyrics, each syllable of a word has to be separated by a **hyphen** and written below its own note. A continuous or dotted line after a syllable shows that it continues for more than one note. Often these notes are also joined by a slur.

## Purcell: *Rejoice in the Lord alway* (for choir)

The second syllable of "re-joice" is stressed, so is on the first beat of the measure.

The dotted rhythm helps the music sound lively and joyful.

The word "Lord" is on the highest note in the opening few measures, which helps to emphasize it.

Slur. Tells you the notes are sung to one syllable.

Re - joice in the Lord al - way and a -

Hyphen. Separates syllables within a word.

Line. Tells you there is more than one note for this syllable.

gain I say re - joice, re -

The slow half notes on "al-way" add emphasis.

## Morley: *Out of the deep* (for alto solo and choir)

The tune starts low and moves upward, mirroring the words "Out of the deep".

Out of the deep have I call - ed to thee, O Lord.

The word "Lord" comes on the highest note.

## Open and short scores

Lots of choir music is for four types of voices: soprano, alto, tenor and bass. This combination is often known by the first letter of each voice: **SATB**. There are two main ways of writing an SATB score: with the music for each voice on a separate staff (called an **open score**), or with two voices sharing a staff (a **short score**). If the voices have similar rhythms, it is often easier to write them in a short score, but if the voices are more complicated, an open score is clearer.

In an SATB short score, the soprano and alto lines go on the top staff, and the tenor and bass lines on the bottom staff. The stems of the soprano and tenor notes all go up, and the stems of the alto and bass notes all go down.

In an open score, the tenor line is written in the treble clef, an octave higher than it sounds (see page 5). In a short score, it shares a staff with the bass line, so it is written in the bass clef, and at the pitch it sounds.

In both open and short scores, an accidental only affects the voice in which it is written. For example, an E flat in the alto line does not affect an E later in the same measure in the soprano line, even if both lines share a staff.

Tallis is most famous for his choral music, written for church services. One is for 40 different voices.

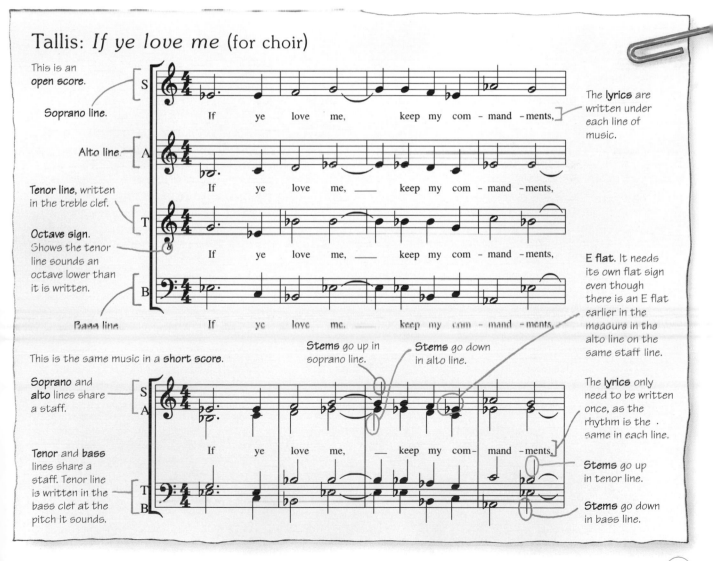

Tallis: *If ye love me* (for choir)

This is an open score.

Soprano line.

Alto line.

Tenor line, written in the treble clef.

Octave sign. Shows the tenor line sounds an octave lower than it is written.

Bass line

The lyrics are written under each line of music.

E flat. It needs its own flat sign even though there is an E flat earlier in the measure in the alto line on the same staff line.

This is the same music in a short score.

Soprano and alto lines share a staff.

Tenor and bass lines share a staff. Tenor line is written in the bass clef at the pitch it sounds.

Stems go up in soprano line.

Stems go down in alto line.

The lyrics only need to be written once, as the rhythm is the same in each line.

Stems go up in tenor line.

Stems go down in bass line.

# HOW INSTRUMENTS DEVELOPED

Instruments have been developing over hundreds of years. Modern instruments often have a louder sound and can play more notes than older versions. Some musicians today use old instruments, or copies of them, to re-create the sound of pieces when they were first performed.

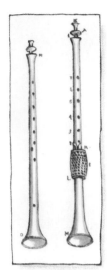

The instruments in these 17th-century drawings are shawms, from which the oboe developed.

## The violin

The first violins were made in the 16th century. They developed from earlier bowed stringed instruments including the rebec.

The greatest violin maker, known as Stradivarius, made over a thousand violins in the late 17th and early 18th centuries. Many famous violinists today use violins which he made.

The rebec was often held in the player's lap.

A sketch by Stradivarius of the top part of a violin

## The piano

The most popular keyboard instrument before the piano was invented was the harpsichord. This has little leather flaps, called plectrums, which pluck the strings. The sound stays the same however hard you press the keys.

This woman is playing a small type of harpsichord, called a virginal.

This oboe was made in the 18th century. It has two keys.

The first pianos, made in the early 18th century, were called fortepianos. They used hammers to hit the strings, and could play loudly and quietly. However, they were much quieter than modern pianos, and had fewer keys.

This picture shows a fortepiano made in 1776.

## Wind instruments

Until the late 1600s, flutes had finger holes but no keys. Adding keys gave extra notes and improved the tuning.

The standard flute used today uses a system of keys and levers invented by a flute player called Boehm in the 19th century. Similar improvements were made to oboes, clarinets and bassoons.

An 18th-century flute with one key

A flute made by Boehm

In the 19th century, valves to open and close pieces of tubing were added to horns and trumpets, creating extra notes.

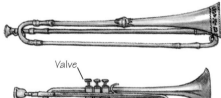

A 17th-century trumpet

Valve

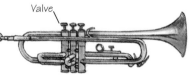

A modern trumpet

# Orchestras

Orchestras (large groups of instruments) began to develop in the 16th century. The number and type of instruments varied from place to place. By the 18th century, most consisted of stringed instruments, with a few wind players and a harpsichord. The harpsichord player or a violinist would direct the orchestra.

This picture shows an 18th-century orchestra directed by the harpsichord player.

As more instruments were invented or improved they were added to the orchestra, and eventually the harpsichord was dropped. Today, some orchestras contain over a hundred players.

The picture below shows you which instruments you might find in a typical modern orchestra, and how they are arranged.

# Electric and electronic instruments

An electric guitar

Pick-up

Instruments which use electricity developed in the 20th century. Electric instruments use electricity to make them sound louder. Electronic instruments need electricity to make sounds at all.

Electric guitars use microphones, called pick-ups, to convert sounds into electric signals. These are fed into an amplifier and converted back into sounds which come out of a loudspeaker. Almost all electronic instruments store sounds digitally (as patterns of numbers or digits) in a tiny part called a microprocessor. On an electronic keyboard, you choose which sounds you want to play by pressing buttons.

This picture shows the first real electric guitar, made in 1931. It became known as the Rickenbacker frying pan because of its long neck and round body.

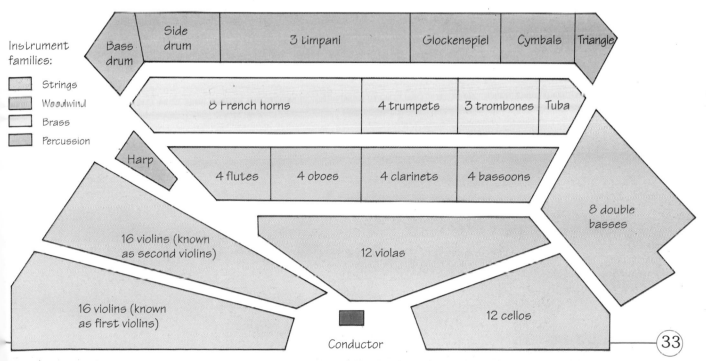

Instrument families:

- Strings
- Woodwind
- Brass
- Percussion

Bass drum | Side drum | 3 timpani | Glockenspiel | Cymbals | Triangle

8 French horns | 4 trumpets | 3 trombones | Tuba

Harp | 4 flutes | 4 oboes | 4 clarinets | 4 bassoons | 8 double basses

16 violins (known as second violins) | 12 violas

16 violins (known as first violins) | 12 cellos

Conductor

# CHORDS

A **chord** is two or more notes played or sung at the same time. The way that chords are made up and fit together in music is called **harmony**.

This picture shows St Thomas' Church in Leipzig, where J.S. Bach was in charge of the music.

## Triads

A **triad** is a chord with three notes in it. The note it is based on is called the **root**. The other notes are a 3rd and a 5th above the root. A triad is named after the word for its root (tonic, supertonic, and so on). This depends on the key of the music. Numbers are often used (1 for tonic, 2 for supertonic, and so on). The numbers are written in Roman numerals (I=1, II=2, III=3, IV=4, V=5, VI=6, VII=7).

In C major, a triad based on D is a supertonic triad (II).

In D minor, a triad based on D is a tonic triad (I).

In G major, a triad based on D is a dominant triad (V).

Depending on the intervals between the root and the other notes, triads are major, minor, augmented or diminished.

A **major triad** consists of a major 3rd and a perfect 5th.

A **minor triad** consists of a minor 3rd and a perfect 5th.

A **diminished triad** consists of a minor 3rd and a diminished 5th.

An **augmented triad** consists of a major 3rd and an augmented 5th.

This manuscript is of a chorale prelude by J.S. Bach. A chorale is a type of hymn. Bach's chorales are admired for their harmony.

Below you can see all the triads based on a C major scale. The pattern of major, minor and diminished triads is the same in every major key.

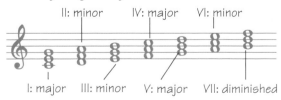

II: minor   IV: major   VI: minor

I: major   III: minor   V: major   VII: diminished

Can you write out the triads Ic, IVb and V in the keys of D major, B flat major and G minor, using the treble clef with key signatures?

The pattern of triads based on a C harmonic minor scale is different.

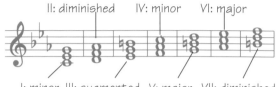

II: diminished   IV: minor   VI: major

I: minor   III: augmented   V: major   VII: diminished

## Inversions

When a triad is written so the root is the lowest note, the triad is in **root position**. If the notes are rewritten so the 3rd is the lowest note, the triad is in **first inversion**. If the 5th is the lowest note, the triad is in **second inversion**.

Root position   First inversion   Second inversion

A letter after a triad's number tells you its inversion. An **a** means root position, **b** means first inversion and **c** means second inversion. For example, Vc is a second inversion dominant triad. If there is no letter, the triad is in root position.

## Close and open position

When a triad is in **close position**, the interval from the lowest note to the highest note is less than an octave.

In **open position**, the middle note of the triad is written an octave higher than usual, so the interval from the lowest to the highest note is greater than an octave. The inversion still depends on which note is the lowest. The triads below are in open position.

Root position   First inversion   Second inversion

## Chords with more notes

In lots of music, chords have more than three notes. They are based on triads, but often with one or more notes repeated in different octaves. A chord is named after the triad it is based on. So to figure out the name of a chord, write it as a triad in close position, keeping the lowest note the same.

This chord is based on a first inversion triad with the root A. In the key of D major it is a Vb chord.

This chord is based on a root position triad with the root A. In the key of G minor it is a IIa, or II, chord.

## 7th chords

A **7th chord** contains the note a 7th above the root, as well as the 3rd and 5th. The most common 7th chord is a **dominant 7th** (written V⁷). It is always a major chord, even in a minor key.

If the chord is arranged so the 7th is the lowest note, it is in **third inversion**. This is shown by the letter **d** after its number, for example, V⁷d.

This is a dominant 7th chord, in root position, in the key of C major. The root is G and the 7th is F.

This is a dominant 7th chord, in first inversion, in the key of A minor. The root is E and the 7th is D. The G is G sharp to make it a major chord.

Try covering up the chord names under the piece by J.S. Bach below. Can you figure out what each one is?

---

J.S. Bach: *Du Friedensfürst, Herr Jesu Christ* (chorale)

**Key signature** of A major.

This **root position** chord contains the root twice.

The chord names are written below each chord.

This note is not part of the harmony.

This is a **dominant 7th** chord. The 7th note is D.

This note is not part of the harmony.

I IV VIIb I Vb IVb V⁷b I Ib IVb I IV V I

**Pause mark.** Tells you the note is longer than usual. This also suggests it is the end of a phrase.

This **subdominant** chord also contains a 6th (the note B).

---

## Other chord symbols

In some types of music, musicians make up their own accompaniment, based on **chord symbols**. For example, guitarists often play from chord symbols above a melody. These tell them which chords to use, but not exactly how to play them.

C — Major chord with the root C

A+ — Augmented chord with the root A

Fm — Minor chord with the root F

Go — Diminished chord with the root G

In the 17th and 18th centuries, organ and harpsichord players often made up accompaniments using a system called **figured bass**. This consists of the lowest note in each chord, with numbers showing what inversion the chord is in.

5 / 3 — Root position

6 / 3 — First inversion

6 / 4 — Second inversion

The figured bass on the right shows a first inversion chord with E as the lowest note. So E is the third, the root is C and the other note is G.

6
3

# CADENCES

The end of a musical phrase is called a **cadence**. The music seems to relax. Sometimes the relaxation feels more final than at other times. The sequence of chords used at a cadence helps to create this feeling.

Mendelssohn was composing music at the age of eleven. Later, he also began to organize music festivals, and became an important conductor.

## Types of cadences

There are four main types of chord sequences used at a cadence. Two of these, called **perfect** and **plagal** cadences, end on the tonic chord. They have a final feel, even if they are not at the end of a piece. The other two chord sequences, called **imperfect** and **interrupted** cadences, do not end on the tonic, so they do not make the music sound as though it has finished.

To identify a cadence, you have to figure out what the two chords at the end of the phrase are.

## Perfect cadences

A **perfect** cadence consists of a dominant chord (V) or dominant seventh (V ) followed by a tonic chord (I). It has the strongest final feel of any cadence, especially if the chords are in root position. At the end of a piece, the tonic chord is always in root position.

These pairs of chords form perfect cadences.

## Haydn: *Quadrille* (for piano)

The music is in the key of C major.

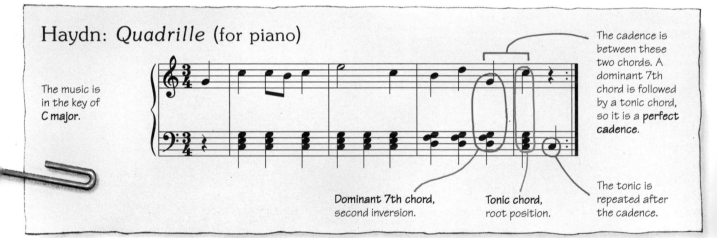

The cadence is between these two chords. A dominant 7th chord is followed by a tonic chord, so it is a **perfect cadence**.

Dominant 7th chord, second inversion.

Tonic chord, root position.

The tonic is repeated after the cadence.

## Plagal cadences

A **plagal** cadence consists of a subdominant chord (IV) followed by a tonic chord (I). It makes a less strong ending than a perfect cadence. Plagal cadences were popular for ending pieces in the 16th century.

Can you figure out the key of each pair of chords in the examples of different cadences on these pages?

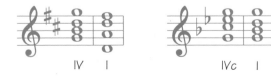

IV    I          IVc    I

These pairs of chords form plagal cadences.

## Imperfect cadences

An **imperfect** cadence ends with a dominant chord (V). The previous chord is often the tonic (I), supertonic (II), subdominant (IV) or submediant (VI). The music sounds as though it is about to continue.

IIb    V          IV    V

These pairs of chords form imperfect cadences.

# Mendelssohn: *Sechs Kinderstücke no.5* (for piano)

The music is in the key of G minor.

The cadence is between these two chords. A subdominant chord is followed by a tonic chord, so it is a **plagal cadence**.

Subdominant chord, second inversion.

Tonic chord, root position.

# Mendelssohn: *Sechs Kinderstücke no.1* (for piano)

The music is in the key of G major.

The cadence is between these two chords. A subdominant chord is followed by a dominant chord, so it is an **imperfect cadence**.

**Dynamic mark.** Stands for *mezzo forte*, which means "moderately loud".

**Dynamic mark.** Stands for sforzando. Tells you to accent this chord.

**Subdominant chord**, root position (the A is a 6th).

**Dominant chord**, root position.

## Interrupted cadences

An **interrupted** cadence begins with a dominant chord (V), so it sounds like the start of a perfect cadence. But the next chord is not the tonic. Often it is the submediant (VI). This sounds unexpected.

V    VI              Vc   VIc

These pairs of chords form interrupted cadences.

# J.S. Bach: *Wachet auf, ruft uns die Stimme* (chorale)

The music is in the key of E flat major.

The cadence is between these two chords. A dominant 7th chord is followed by a submediant chord, so it is an **interrupted cadence**.

**Dominant chord**, root position. The A flat quarter note adds the 7th to make a **dominant 7th chord**.

**Submediant chord**, root position.

# ORNAMENTS

**Ornaments** are notes which decorate a tune. In the past, performers often made up ornaments, but from the 17th century, composers began to indicate them with symbols. There is usually no single correct way to play an ornament.

Schubert often performed his piano music at parties which he gave for his friends. He also wrote over six hundred songs.

## Grace notes

**Grace notes** are usually played very quickly just before the beat. They are written as small eighth notes or sixteenth notes, often joined to the next main note by a slur. A single grace note, called an **acciaccatura**, has a line through it.

When you write grace notes, they do not have any time value. The other notes in the measure add up to a full measure.

## Appogiaturas

An **appogiatura** is written as a small note slurred to a main melody note. It is played on the beat of the main note.

Normally, if the main note divides into two parts, the appogiatura and the main note each last for half its length. If the main note divides into three, then the appogiatura usually lasts for two-thirds of it, and the main note for one third.

Appogiatura

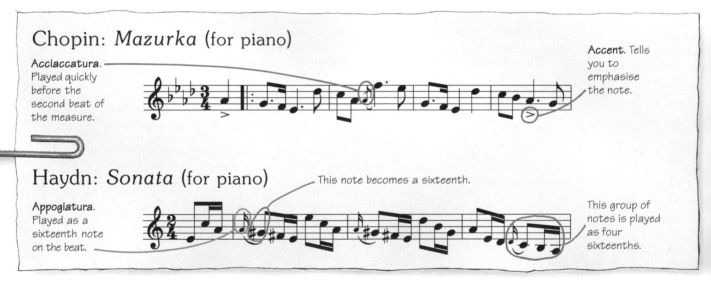

## Chopin: *Mazurka* (for piano)

**Acciaccatura.** Played quickly before the second beat of the measure.

**Accent.** Tells you to emphasise the note.

## Haydn: *Sonata* (for piano)

**Appogiatura.** Played as a sixteenth note on the beat.

This note becomes a sixteenth.

This group of notes is played as four sixteenths.

## Trills

A **trill** is a very quick repeated alternation between the written note and the note above it. Trills usually last for the whole length of the written note. Often the last alternation is with the note below the written note. An accidental above a trill sign applies to the upper note.

Trill signs $\quad$ *tr* $\quad$ *tr*$\sim$ $\qquad$ Upper note is a sharp $\;$ #*tr* $\qquad$ Upper note is a flat $\;$ ♭*tr*

In music written before the 19th century, a trill usually starts on the note above the written note. In music written since then, a trill usually starts on the written note, unless this sounds awkward.

Trill starting on written note

Trill starting on note above written note

## Vivaldi: *The four seasons* (for violin and orchestra)

**Trill** between D and E flat, starting on the upper note (E flat), as the music was written before the 19th century.

In the piece, these trills are supposed to sound like a bird singing.

## Tchaikovsky: *Violin concerto* (for violin and orchestra)

**Trill** between G sharp and A, starting on the written note (G sharp), as the music was written in the 19th century.

**Trill** between A and B flat, with an accent on the first note.

**Dynamic mark.** Stands for fortissimo, which means "very loud".

**Trill** between A and B natural.

This is also a **trill** between A and B natural.

## Mordents

There are two types of mordents, called upper and lower. An **upper mordent** consists of the written note, the note above and the written note again played quickly at the beginning of the beat.

A **lower mordent** uses the note below, not above, the written note.

Upper mordent

Lower mordent

Upper note is a sharp

Lower note is a flat

## Turns

For a **turn** written above a note, play the note above the written note, the written note, the note below, then the written note again. The turn starts on the beat, and lasts for as long as the written note.

For a turn after a note, play the note, then the turn just before the next note.

Turn on the note

Turn after the note

Upper note is a natural

Lower note is a sharp

Brahms gave the manuscript of the violin piece above to a friend to correct. The corrections are in blue.

## Brahms: *Sextet* (for two violins, two violas and two cellos)

**Tenuto mark.** Hold the note for its full length, or a little longer.

**Upper mordent.** Played quickly on the beat: E flat, F, E flat.

**Upper mordent.** Played quickly on the beat: C, D, C.

## Schubert: *Scherzo* (for piano)

This note is played before the turn.

**Turn.** Played on the beat, each note a sixteenth long: C, B flat, A natural, B flat.

**Turn.** Played quickly at the end of the E flat note: F, E flat, D, E flat.

# STRUCTURE

Just as phrases give a melody structure, larger sections of music give structure to a whole piece. The structure of a piece is called its **form**. You can find out about some basic forms on these two pages.

*Telemann wrote more music than almost any other composer.*

## Binary form

A piece in **binary form** divides into two sections. The first section is answered by the second section. Rhythms or melodies in the first section may be echoed or developed in the second. The first section may modulate (see page 29) to another key. The second section may end back in the original key. Often, both sections are repeated.

## Telemann: *Fantasia* (for flute)

This music is in **binary form**. It has two sections, both of which are repeated.

Start of **first section**: lasts for 13 measures. It modulates to the dominant: B major.

Start of **second section**: lasts 16 measures. It ends back in E major.

The rhythms and melody in the second section echo and vary those in the first section.

## Theme and variations

Pieces in this form begin with a main tune, called the **theme**, which is then changed and decorated in various ways. For example, the notes of the theme may be hidden among other notes, the rhythm may be changed slightly, or the key may be major instead of minor. These different versions of the theme are called **variations**.

## Handel: *Suite in E major* (for keyboard)

This music is a **theme and variations**.

Start of **theme**: main tune is in the top line.

Start of **first variation**: extra notes added.

Start of **second variation**: theme slightly changed, with notes above.

The first two measures are repeated exactly.

This note becomes part of the tune in the first variation.

**Syncopation.** The note comes a sixteenth later than you expect.

The opening is not repeated exactly.

## Rondo form

In **rondo form**, the opening section of music keeps being repeated throughout a piece, with different music (called **episodes**) in between. The episodes may always be the same, or they may vary. Often they contrast with the main tune, or are in a different key. The piece may finish with the main tune again, or with an extra end section called a **coda**.

## Mozart: *Serenade in B flat* (for two oboes, two clarinets, two basset horns, four horns, two bassoons and double bass)

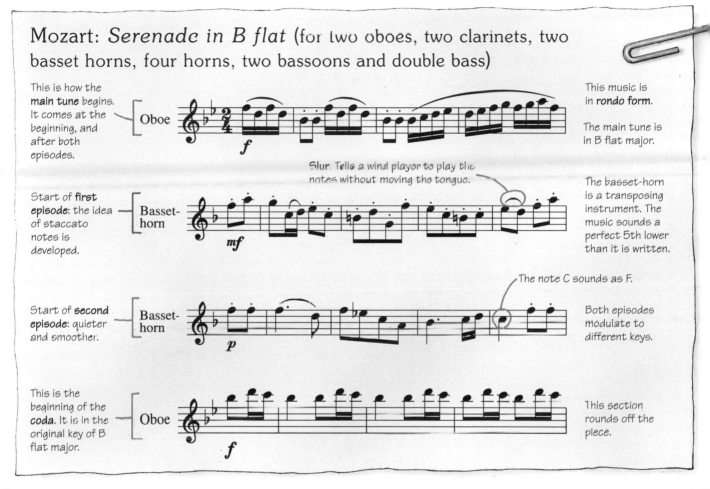

This is how the **main tune** begins. It comes at the beginning, and after both episodes.

Oboe

This music is in rondo form.

The main tune is in B flat major.

Slur. Tells a wind player to play the notes without moving the tongue.

Start of **first episode**: the idea of staccato notes is developed.

Basset-horn

The basset-horn is a transposing instrument. The music sounds a perfect 5th lower than it is written.

The note C sounds as F.

Start of **second episode**: quieter and smoother.

Basset-horn

Both episodes modulate to different keys.

This is the beginning of the **coda**. It is in the original key of B flat major.

Oboe

This section rounds off the piece.

## Larger structures

Long pieces are often divided into big sections, with short pauses between.

Some examples of these larger structures are **symphonies** (for orchestra), **concertos** (for soloist and orchestra), **sonatas** (for soloist and, often, piano) and **chamber music** (for small groups of instruments). The music usually divides into three or four sections called **movements**. Each movement has its own basic form, but is also part of the overall structure of the piece. Often, themes and ideas are developed or repeated between movements. There are usually strong contrasts of speed or mood too.

**Suites** are collections of pieces, often dances, which usually contrast in speed and style. For example, some may be fast and lively, others slow and stately.

Long **choral** pieces and **operas** usually divide into separate sections. The form of these sections often depends on the meaning and structure of the lyrics. In opera, the action on stage also affects the form of the music.

Handel played the organ and violin. His main interests were in opera and choral music.

# SCALE CHART

You can find out about other types of scales on page 17.

Below is a chart of scales, written with key signatures. Each major scale appears with its relative minors. The names of these pairs of relative major and minor keys are shown down the side of each page. Major and harmonic minor scales are only shown ascending, as the notes are the same in the descending version.

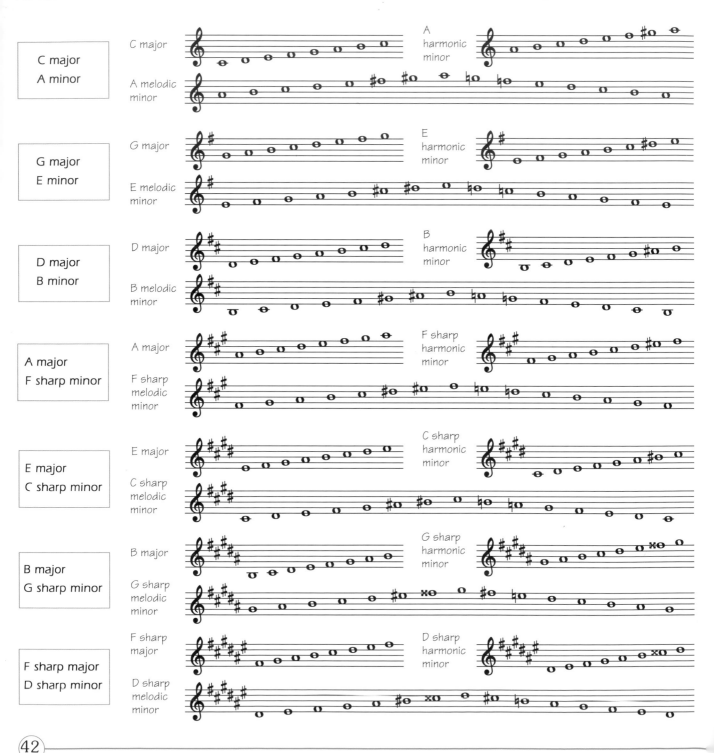

C major
A minor

G major
E minor

D major
B minor

A major
F sharp minor

E major
C sharp minor

B major
G sharp minor

F sharp major
D sharp minor

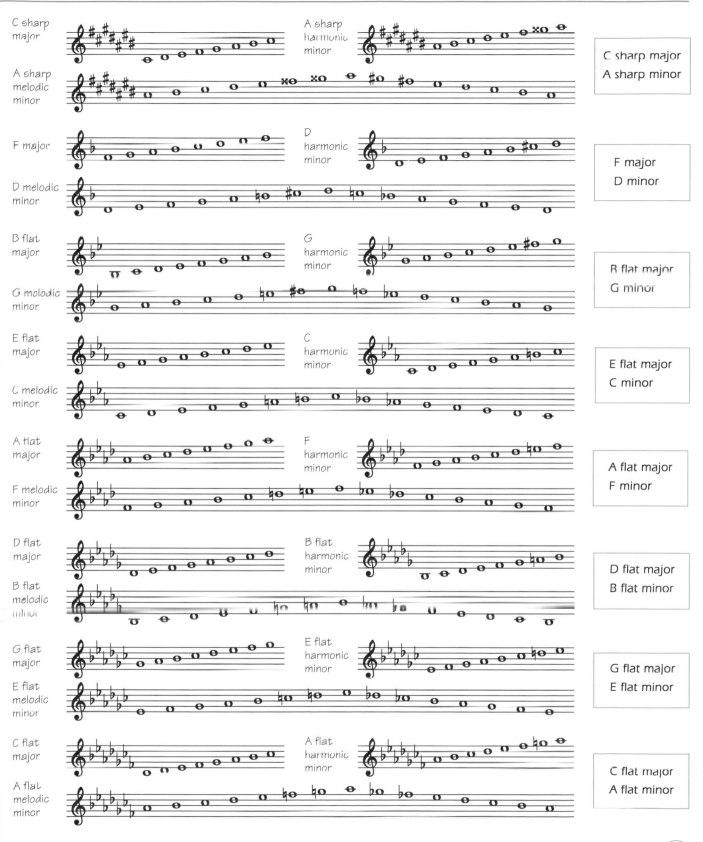

# MUSICAL TERMS

Music was first printed in Italy, so many musical terms are in Italian. Others are in French or German. On these two pages you can find out what some of the most common musical terms mean.

**a capella**  term used for choral music sung without accompaniment

**accelerando, accel.**  get gradually faster (see also **stringendo**)

**adagio**  slow, at a leisurely pace

**ad libitum, ad lib.**  an indication that a passage may be played freely, not strictly in time; or that a note, section or instrument may be left out

**affettuoso**  tenderly, affectionately

**agitato**  agitated, restless, excited

**alla marcia**  in the style of a march

**allargando**  broadening, slowing down; the music usually gets louder and sounds more dignified

**allegretto**  not as fast as **allegro** and in a lighter style

**allegro**  quick, at a lively speed

**amoroso**  loving, affectionate

**andante**  moderately slow, at a walking pace; a bit slower than **moderato**

**andantino**  a little faster and more lighthearted than **andante**; can also mean a little slower than **andante**

**animato**  animated, lively

**appassionato**  passionately

**arco**  an instruction to string players to bow the strings (used after **pizzicato**)

**assai**  very (**allegro assai** means very fast)

**a tempo**  an indication to return to the original speed after a change in speed, such as **rit.**, **rall.**, **accel.**

**attacca**  attack; instruction to go straight on to the next section without a pause (see also **segue**)

**calando**  getting quieter, dying away; often means slowing down as well

**calmato**  calmly

**cantabile**  in a singing style

**col legno**  an instruction to play a stringed instrument with the wood of the bow rather than with the hair

**con brio**  vigorously, with spirit

**con ped.**  with pedal; instruction to pianists to use the sustaining pedal

**con sordino**  with mute

**crescendo, cresc.**  gradually getting louder (opposite of **decrescendo**)

**da capo, D.C.,**  indication that the music is to be repeated from the beginning

**da capo al fine**, repeat from the beginning and end at the word **fine**

**dal segno**  repeat from the sign ％

**dal segno al fine**, repeat from the sign ％ and end at the word **fine**

**decrescendo, decresc.**  gradually getting quieter (see also **diminuendo**; opposite of **crescendo**)

**delicato**  delicately

**détaché**  detached; string players should play each note with a separate stroke of the bow

**diminuendo, dim.**  gradually getting quieter (see also **decrescendo**)

**divisi, div.**  an indication to one section within a group of players (usually strings) to divide into two or more groups, each playing a different part

**dolce**  sweetly

**en animant**  becoming more animated and lively

**espressivo**  expressively

**fine**  end

**forte**  loud, strong

**fortepiano**  loud, then immediately quiet

**fortissimo**  very loud

**giusto**  exact, strict (**tempo giusto** means in strict time)

**glissando**  instruction to slide from one pitch to another some distance away (for example, by sliding along the keys of a piano, or the strings of a harp)

**grave**  very slow, serious

**joyeux**  joyful, cheerful

**laisser vibrer**  leave to vibrate; do not damp; allow the sound to continue

**larghetto**  fairly slow and broad, but not as slow as **largo**

**largo**  broad, at a slow stately speed

**legato**  smooth (opposite of **staccato**)

**leggiero**  light and nimble

**lento**  slow

**loco**  indicates a return to the normal pitch after an octave sign

**maestoso**  majestic

**marcato**  marked, stressed, accented

**meno**  less (**meno forte** means less loud)

**mezzo forte**  moderately loud

**mezzo piano**  moderately quiet

**misterioso**  mysteriously

**moderato**  at a moderate speed

**molto**  much, very (**molto allegro** means very fast)

**morendo**  dying away

**mosso**  with motion

**nobilmente**  nobly

**obbligato**  necessary; usually refers to an instrument which cannot be left out

**ottava**  octave (**ottava bassa** means octave lower, **ottava alta** means octave higher)

**pesante**  heavy, weighty

**pianissimo**  very quiet

**piano**  quiet

**più**  more (**più mosso** means more motion, more quickly)

**pizzicato**  plucked; an indication to string players to pluck the strings with the fingertips rather than bow them

**placido**  peaceful, calm

**poco**  little, somewhat (**poco a poco** means little by little, gradually; **poco lento** means somewhat slow)

**presto**  quick, fast; faster than **allegro**

**prima, primo**  first (**tempo primo** means first speed, the speed used at the beginning of the piece)

**quasi**  in the style of; almost; as though

**rallentando, rall.**  gradually getting slower (see also **ritardando**)

**ritardando, rit.**  gradually getting slower (see also **rallentando**)

**rubato, tempo rubato**  not strictly in time, linger on certain notes

**sans**  without

**scherzando**  jokingly, playfully

**schnell**  quick

**sec, secco**  crisp, short and detached (see also **staccato**); instruction to damp the sound immediately

**secondo**  second (**seconda volta** means second time)

**segue**  go on to the next section or piece immediately; continue in the same style (see also **attacca**)

**sempre**  always, continually

**senza ped.**  without pedal

**sforzando**  forced, strongly accented

**simile, sim.**  same, similar; continue in a similar style or manner

**smorzando**  dying away; getting slower and quieter

**sostenuto**  sustained

**spiccato**  detached; instruction to string players to bounce the bow off the strings, using short, crisp strokes

**spiritoso**  spirited, lively

**staccatissimo**  very short

**staccato**  short, detached (see also **sec**; opposite of **legato**)

**stringendo**  hurrying; gradually getting faster (see also **accelerando**)

**subito, sub.**  suddenly (**subito forte** means suddenly loud)

**sul ponticello**  an indication to string players to bow the strings close to, or on, the bridge

**sul tasto**  an instruction to string players to bow the strings close to, or over, the end of the fingerboard

**tempo**  speed

**tenuto**  held; tells you to hold the note or chord for its full time value, or even a little longer

**tremolando**  trembling, quivering; a note is repeated very rapidly, or several notes are alternated

**troppo**  too much, too (**allegro, ma non troppo** means fast, but not too much)

**tutti**  all; everyone playing together

**una corda**  an instruction to pianists to use the left, or "soft", pedal

**unisono, unis.**  two or more voices or instruments sounding the same pitch; a direction to cancel **divisi**

**vigoroso**  vigorous, strong

**vivace**  lively, quick

**volante**  fast and light

**volti subito, V.S.**  instruction to turn the page immediately

# SYMBOLS

Below you can see some of the most common musical signs and symbols. Page numbers next to them tell you where in the book you can find out more, or see an example in an extract from a famous piece.

| | | | |
|---|---|---|---|
| *8va* | Octave sign, or ottava alta (see pages 5, 45) | *p* | Piano (see pages 7, 45) |
| *8va* | Octave sign, or ottava bassa (see pages 7, 45) | *pp* | Pianissimo (see page 45) |
| | | *mp* | Mezzo piano (see page 45) |
| | Treble, or G, clef (see page 4) | *sf* | Sforzando (see page 37, 45) |
| | Bass, or F, clef (see page 6) | | Down bow (see page 6) |
| | Alto, or C, clef (see page 6) | V | Up bow (see page 6) |
| | Tenor, or C, clef (see page 6) | ' | Breath mark (see pages 4, 29) |
| | Treble clef sounding one octave lower than written (see page 5, 31) | | Tie (see pages 9, 10) |
| | | | Slur (see pages 6, 8, 41) |
| ♯ | Sharp (see page 14) | | Staccato (see pages 8, 45) |
| ♭ | Flat (see page 14) | | Pause (see pages 15, 35) |
| ♮ | Natural (see page 14) | | Tenuto (see pages 29, 45) |
| 𝄪 | Double sharp (see page 15) | | Accent (see page 38) |
| ♭♭ | Double flat (see page 15) | | Repeat signs (see page 15) |
| | Time signature (see pages 10, 20, 21) | 𝄋 | Segno (see page 44) |
| **C** | Common time (see page 10) | | Spread chord (see page 17) |
| **¢** | Alla breve (see page 10) | *tr* *tr*⌇ | Trills (see page 38) |
| | Crescendo (see pages 7, 44) | ∿ | Upper mordent (see page 39) |
| | Decrescendo (see pages 7, 44) | ∿ | Lower mordent (see page 39) |
| *f* | Forte (see pages 8, 44) | | Appoggiatura (see page 38) |
| *ff* | Fortissimo (see pages 39, 44) | | Acciaccatura (see page 38) |
| *mf* | Mezzo forte (see pages 37, 45) | ∾ | Turn (see page 39) |

# ANSWERS

## Page 5

The notes in the music by Corelli on page 4 are: A, E, E, A, A, B, C, B, C, D, B, C, A, F, F, E, E, A, D, E, E.

## Page 7

The notes in the first line of music by J.S. Bach on page 6 are: E, F, G, C, B, C, C, chord of G, D, B (lowest note first), A, B, G, D, E, F, B, A, B, G, chord of C, G, F (lowest note first), E, D, E, C, C, B.

## Page 10

This is how you write two sixteenth notes beamed to an eighth note:

The time signature $\frac{3}{2}$ means there are three half beats in a measure.

The time signature $\frac{6}{4}$ means there are six quarter beats in a measure.

The time signature $\frac{12}{8}$ means there are twelve eighth beats in a measure.

## Page 16

D major scale in the bass clef.

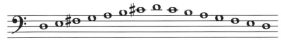

D harmonic minor scale in the bass clef:

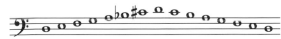

D melodic minor scale in the bass clef:

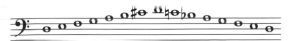

## Page 18

D major scale with its key signature in the bass clef:

D harmonic minor scale with its key signature in the bass clef:

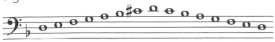

D melodic minor scale with its key signature in the bass clef:

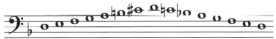

A sentence starting with the names of the sharps in the correct order: Furious Camels Give Dangerous Adders Enormous Bites.

A sentence starting with the names of the flats in the correct order: Blue Elephant Airways Do Give Comfortable Flights.

## Page 24

The note a minor 7th above G is F.
The note an augmented 4th above G is C sharp.
The note a perfect 12th above G is D.

## Page 26

This is the clarinet part of the music by Beethoven on page 27, written as it sounds:

## Page 34

These are the triads in D major:

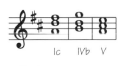

These are the triads in B flat major:

These are the triads in G minor:

(If you have written exactly these chords in another octave, your answers are correct.)

## Page 36

The keys of the pairs of chords are:
Perfect cadences: F major, A minor
Plagal cadences: D major, G minor
Imperfect cadences: C major, D minor
Interrupted cadences: C major, E minor.

# INDEX

First published in 1996 by Usborne Publishing Ltd, Usborne House, 83-85 Saffron Hill, London EC1N 8RT, England. Copyright © 1996 Usborne Publishing Ltd. The name Usborne and the device are Trade Marks of Usborne Publishing Ltd. All rights reserved. No part of this publication may be reproduced, stored in a retrieval system or transmitted in any form or by any means, electronic, mechanical, photocopying, recording or otherwise, without the prior permission of the publisher. First published in America in March 1997. AE. Printed in Spain.